GRADE **5**

# Reader's and Writer's JOURNAL

Glenview, Illinois • Boston, Massachusetts • Chandler, Arizona • Hoboken, New Jersey

ISBN-13: 978-0-328-85160-7
ISBN-10:    0-328-85160-4

6   16

# Table of Contents

# Table of Contents

# Table of Contents

Name _____

**DIRECTIONS** Write a sentence using each word.

claimed    experiment    species

_____

_____

_____

_____

**Write in Response to Reading**

Reread pages 1 and 2 and pages 5 and 6. Think about how the characters Ben and Frankie speak and act. Use details from the book to compare and contrast their words and actions. Write your answer below, on a separate sheet of paper, or in a new document.

_____

_____

_____

_____

_____

Students demonstrate contextual understanding of Benchmark Vocabulary. Students read text closely and use text evidence in their written answers.

Name _____

## Suffix *-ly*

**DIRECTIONS** On the line, write the base word of the underlined word.

1. The pillows suit the new couch quite <u>nicely</u>. _____

2. The cat <u>completely</u> destroyed the old couch. _____

3. The material on the new one is more <u>securely</u> sewn. _____

4. We have <u>diligently</u> tried to keep the cat off of it. _____

5. The dog <u>happily</u> has the couch to itself. _____

**DIRECTIONS** Turn the adjective on the left into an adverb by adding *-ly*. Then use the adverb in a sentence with the verb on the right.

6. constant     rains       _____

7. original     lived       _____

8. private      discuss     _____

9. usual        eat         _____

10. merry       sang        _____

11. unfair      criticized  _____

12. mysterious  appeared    _____

13. beautiful   grow        _____

14. kind        speak       _____

15. thorough    read        _____

Students apply grade-level phonics and word analysis skills.

**Compare and Contrast Characters** On a separate sheet of paper or in a new document, write two paragraphs to compare and contrast two characters from the story. First, choose two characters to compare and contrast. Find descriptions of each character's traits, thoughts, feelings, words, and actions. Write about one character in each paragraph.

## Common and Proper Nouns

**DIRECTIONS** Circle the common nouns and underline the proper nouns in these sentences.

The rattlesnakes he used to watch were at the Desert Museum in Tucson, Arizona.

In December, his dad was offered a new job, and two months later his family left Tucson for Massachusetts.

Students write routinely for a range of tasks, purposes, and audiences. Students practice various conventions of standard English.

Name _____

**DIRECTIONS** Write a sentence using each word.

ecosystems        biomes

_____

_____

_____

_____

**Write in Response to Reading**

Reread the fifth paragraph on p. 21. Use details from the book to write an informative paragraph explaining what a *terrarium* is. Write your answer below, on a separate sheet of paper, or in a new document.

_____

_____

_____

_____

_____

_____

 Students demonstrate contextual understanding of Benchmark Vocabulary. Students read text closely and use text evidence in their written answers.

Name _____

## Sentence Structure and Sensory Details

**DIRECTIONS** Reread the last three full paragraphs on p. 30 of *Night of the Spadefoot Toads*.

1. What sensory words and phrases does the author use to help you visualize the setting?

   _____

   _____

2. Explain how these words and phrases help you understand how Ben feels physically in that setting.

   _____

   _____

3. What sensory words and phrases does the author use to show you what Ben's father is like?

   _____

   _____

4. Explain how these words help you understand Ben's father.

   _____

   _____

5. What do you notice about the sentence structure in these paragraphs?

   _____

   _____

6. What is the effect of this structure on your impression of Ben's father?

   _____

   _____

Students analyze and respond to literary and informational text.

**Analyze Craft and Style** Choose a 5–10 line passage from Chapter 2 or 3, and write several paragraphs analyzing the author's craft and style. Make sure each paragraph has a clear topic, and use examples from the text to develop the topic and support your analysis and interpretation. Consider the author's choices, including sentence length, word choice, and sensory details. Write about how these choices create particular effects and convey meaning. Use a separate sheet of paper or start a new document.

**Conventions**

## Abstract Nouns

**DIRECTIONS** On a separate sheet of paper or in a new document, rewrite two consecutive paragraphs from Chapter 2 or 3. Add abstract nouns to both paragraphs, but be sure to keep the original meaning of the text.

 Students write routinely for a range of tasks, purposes, and audiences. Students practice various conventions of standard English.

**DIRECTIONS** Write a sentence using each word.

wry    baffled

_____

_____

_____

_____

**Write in Response to Reading**

Write a narrative paragraph from Ryan's perspective. Use third-person point of view to describe what Ryan is thinking and doing during the scene on p. 38 that begins "Ryan's not listening." Include descriptions of Ben from Ryan's perspective. Use evidence from the text to help you write your narrative. Write your answer below, on a separate sheet of paper, or in a new document.

_____

_____

_____

_____

_____

_____

Students demonstrate contextual understanding of Benchmark Vocabulary. Students read text closely and use text evidence in their written answers.

## Fishy Business!

The Columbia River flows westward for more than 1,200 miles (1,931 kilometers) across the Northwest. A paradise for fish, right? At one time, it was. Yet when humans decided to control the water rushing to the ocean, no one asked the fish what they thought.

A dam is a man-made structure built across a river. Dams both help prevent flooding and provide water for irrigation. Larger dams generate pollution-free and inexpensive hydroelectric power. Over time, more than four hundred dams have been built along the Columbia River, eleven of which extend completely across the river.

Consider, however, how these dams affect the natural environment, specifically the salmon living in these waters. Salmon make only two long journeys during their lives. Hatched in rivers far from the ocean, young salmon swim to the ocean where they spend their adult lives. Near the end of their lives, they swim back to their birthplace. In the cool streams, females lay eggs, and males fertilize them.

What happens when a young fish swimming toward the ocean encounters a dam that crosses the entire river? Water stored behind the dam rushes downward through chutes and turns huge turbines to generate electricity. Spinning blades are not a healthy environment for fish!

If the fish somehow makes it to the ocean, it must eventually swim upstream against the current to reach its spawning ground. Fish can do this for long distances when the slope is gentle. However, climbing a dam more than 100 feet (30 meters) high is quite a challenge! Because dams make it difficult for fish to spawn, salmon and trout populations along the Columbia River have dropped from 16 million to 2.5 million.

Since the 1930s, builders have added "fishways" such as fish ladders to dams. A fish ladder is a series of gradually ascending pools next to a dam that are filled with rushing water. The fish swim upriver against the current, leaping from a lower pool to a higher one. They rest in the pool before repeating the process until they are above the dam.

Fish ladders and other structures are like elevators. They fill with fish, rise to the top of the dam, and open to let the fish out. They can add millions of dollars to a dam's cost, but isn't the expense worth it? Causing whole populations of fish to die out is unthinkable. Preserving the environment is priceless.

 Students read text closely to determine what the text says.

**Gather Evidence** On p. 8, circle the paragraph that contains three ways that dams in the Northwest have helped residents of the area. Underline the three details.

**Gather Evidence: Extend Your Ideas** Briefly explain why the details are important to the article.

_____

_____

**Ask Questions** Write three questions about salmon near the Columbia River that are answered in the text or by the images. Circle questions and answers in the text. Use one color for the first questions and answer, a second color for the second, and so on.

_____

_____

_____

**Ask Questions: Extend Your Ideas** Were any of the questions in the text left unanswered? If the answer is yes, explain.

_____

_____

**Make Your Case** On p. 8, draw a box around details the writer uses to describe the structures built to help the fish. Then underline the writer's strongest supportive details.

 Students read text closely to determine what the text says.

Name _____

**Analyze Narrator Point of View** Choose a passage from Chapter 4 or 5 that describes a story event from Ben's point of view. Consider how the event might be described if it were told from the point of view of a different character, such as the frog or Mrs. Tibbets. Write at least three paragraphs that present the story event from this character's point of view, describing the character's thoughts and feelings about the situation or event. Use a separate sheet of paper or start a new document.

**Conventions**

## Plural, Singular, and Collective Nouns

**DIRECTIONS** Write a sentence that uses the noun type identified as its subject.

1. Singular Noun _____

   _____

2. Plural Noun _____

   _____

3. Collective Noun (singular) _____

   _____

4. Collective Noun (plural) _____

   _____

 Students write routinely for a range of tasks, purposes, and audiences. Students practice various conventions of standard English.

Name _____

**DIRECTIONS** Write a sentence using each word.

deflated    marvel    vernal

_____

_____

_____

_____

**Write in Response to Reading**

Reread pages 74 and 75. Although Ben remembers that Mrs. Tibbets told him "Don't go near the cage," he ignores her warning. Think about what you know about Ben. Why do you think he is so interested in the snake cage? Why do you think he lies and tells Mrs. Tibbets that he did not bother the snakes? Write your answer below, on a separate sheet of paper, or in a new document.

_____

_____

_____

_____

_____

Students demonstrate contextual
understanding of Benchmark Vocabulary.
Students read text closely and use text
evidence in their written answers.

## Plot

**DIRECTIONS** Using evidence from the text, answer the following questions about Chapters 6 and 7 from *Night of the Spadefoot Toads*.

1.  Who are the characters in Chapters 6 and 7?

    _____

    _____

2.  What are the settings in Chapters 6 and 7?

    _____

    _____

3.  What is the main conflict, or problem, of Chapter 6?

    _____

    _____

4.  What are the most important events in Chapter 6? Why are they important?

    _____

    _____

5.  What is the main conflict, or problem, of Chapter 7?

    _____

    _____

6.  What are the most important events in Chapter 7? Why are they important?

    _____

    _____

Students analyze and respond to literary and informational text.

**Establish a Situation** Write one page of a short story. Establish a situation using *Night of the Spadefoot Toads* as a model. Introduce and give brief background information about each main character, introduce a narrator, and establish a sequence of events. Consider your purpose (to entertain) and your audience (other students) as you write your narrative. Use a separate sheet of paper or start a new document.

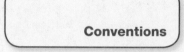

**Conventions**

### Pronouns

**DIRECTIONS** Write a sentence that includes the type of pronoun identified. Then underline each example of that type of pronoun in your sentence.

1. Personal Pronoun _____

_____

2. Possessive Pronoun _____

_____

3. Relative Pronoun _____

_____

4. Indefinite Pronoun _____

_____

 Students write routinely for a range of tasks, purposes, and audiences. Students practice various conventions of standard English.

Name _____

**DIRECTIONS** Write a sentence using each word.

extinct       careens

_____

_____

_____

_____

**Write in Response to Reading**

Reread the last full paragraph on p. 101. Write a diary entry as though you were Ben just after he arrived home from Mrs. Tibbets's house. Explain what has happened and what you are thinking and feeling. Write about what motivated you to behave the way you did with Mrs. Tibbets. Be sure to base your diary entry on details from the text. Write your answer on a separate sheet of paper or in a new document.

_____

_____

_____

_____

_____

_____

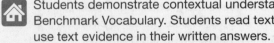

Students demonstrate contextual understanding of Benchmark Vocabulary. Students read text closely and use text evidence in their written answers.

**Develop a Character** On a separate sheet of paper or in a new document, write 2–3 paragraphs that develop a character's traits, feelings or thoughts, and responses to events. Use concrete words or phrases and sensory details to develop the characters you introduced in Lesson 4.

**Conventions**

## Personal Pronouns

**DIRECTIONS** On the line next to each sentence, write a personal pronoun that could replace each underlined word or group of words.

1. Rattlesnakes can be dangerous, so people should be careful around <u>the animals</u>. _____

2. <u>Caroline</u> went to France with her family last year. ____

3. <u>Marcus and I</u> have been friends for more than fifteen years. ____

4. The tour guide told <u>John</u> a lot of interesting facts about <u>the house</u>. _____

5. <u>The movie</u> was very boring, so <u>the boys</u> left early. _____

Students write routinely for a range of tasks, purposes, and audiences. Students practice various conventions of standard English.

**Unit 1 • Module A • Lesson 5 • 15**

## Greek and Latin Roots

### Greek Root Bank

| | | |
|---|---|---|
| *techno*, skill | *hydro*, water | *phon*, sound |
| *micro*, small | *therm*, heat | *bio*, life |

### Latin Root Bank

| | | |
|---|---|---|
| *oper*, work | *brevis*, short | *aqua*, water |
| *multi*, many | *rupt*, break | *aud*, hear |

**DIRECTIONS** Use the Word Banks to find the root related to each underlined word. Write the root on the line. You may not use all of the roots, and some roots may appear more than once.

1. He spoke so quietly that his words were barely <u>audible</u>. _____

2. I was very glad that the speech was <u>brief</u>. _____

3. There is a bright red fire <u>hydrant</u> near my house. _____

4. She used a <u>thermometer</u> to test the candy. _____

5. Would you please turn your cell <u>phone</u> off now? _____

6. We took a field trip to the <u>aquarium</u> yesterday. _____

7. Everyone in the <u>audience</u> rose for the standing ovation. _____

8. Maria Callas was a famous <u>opera</u> singer. _____

9. Ben Franklin wrote a lengthy <u>autobiography</u>. _____

10. Drawing a flower in detail requires a good <u>technique</u>. _____

11. Please don't cause a <u>disruption</u> in the cafeteria. _____

 Students apply grade-level phonics and word analysis skills.

Name _____

**DIRECTIONS** Write a sentence using each word.

straggle    welling    dwindled    feebly

_____

_____

_____

_____

_____

_____

**Write in Response to Reading**

Reread the story on p. 129 that Mrs. Tibbets tells Ben about the Overtoad. Write a story using all of the animals that Ben and Mrs. Tibbets find the night they look for the spadefoot toads. Include details about the setting and how it influences the Overtoad appearing on this special night. Write your answer on a separate sheet of paper or in a new document.

_____

_____

_____

_____

_____

_____

Students demonstrate contextual understanding of Benchmark Vocabulary. Students read text closely and use text evidence in their written answers.

Name _____

**Develop a Sequence of Events** On a separate sheet of paper or in a new document, write 2–3 paragraphs that develop a natural sequence of events using your narrative from Lessons 4 and 5. Organize your story into a beginning, middle, and end, and include transitions to show a sequence of events. Remember that events should relate to characters' responses to a conflict.

**Conventions**

## Possessive Pronouns

**DIRECTIONS** Underline the possessive pronoun in each sentence.

1. Frankie has the jar in his hands.

2. "Sit in your seats," the teacher says.

3. Its feet are shaped like spades.

4. Pamela took her dog to the veterinarian.

5. We visited our grandparents yesterday.

 Students write routinely for a range of tasks, purposes, and audiences. Students practice various conventions of standard English.

Name _____

**DIRECTIONS** Write a sentence using each word.

inherited    sinister    query    murky

_____

_____

_____

_____

**Write in Response to Reading**

Reread the fifth full paragraph on p. 152. Do you think Ben's impression of Mrs. Tibbets is correct? State your opinion, and support it using evidence from the text. Write your answer on a separate sheet of paper or in a new document.

_____

_____

_____

_____

_____

_____

Students demonstrate contextual understanding of Benchmark Vocabulary. Students read text closely and use text evidence in their written answers.

**Style**

**DIRECTIONS** Answer the following questions about Chapter 12 of *Night of the Spadefoot Toads.*

1. Why does the author use italics on pp. 140–142? How do they help you understand the story?

   _____

   _____

2. What phrases does the author repeat on p. 140? Why do you think the author repeated these phrases?

   _____

   _____

   _____

   _____

3. Why do you think the author uses the phrase "scream bloody murder" on p. 153?

   _____

   _____

   _____

4. How does the use of exclamation points on pp. 152–153 add to the meaning of the text?

   _____

5. How does the use of periods to punctuate the words *dead* and *gone* on p. 154 add to the meaning of the text?

   _____

   _____

Students analyze and respond to literary and informational text.

**Develop Setting** On a separate sheet of paper or in a new document, write 1–2 paragraphs that develop a setting for your narrative from the previous lessons. Consider how the setting will influence your characters' actions or create contrast. Include concrete words or phrases and sensory details to help develop your setting.

**Conventions**

### Relative Pronouns

**DIRECTIONS** For each sentence below, add commas if it includes a nonrestrictive clauses or write NC next to the sentence if it includes a restrictive clause that does not need commas.

1.  He talked with Mr. Phillips  who is a science teacher at the local high school.

    _____

2.  The man whom Ben called has not responded yet. _____

3.  She wants to sell the land that surrounds the house. _____

4.  Spadefoot toads  which rely on vernal pools  are endangered in Massachusetts.

    _____

5.  The teacher whose husband inherited the land is not the land's current owner.

    _____

 Students write routinely for a range of tasks, purposes, and audiences. Students practice various conventions of standard English.

**DIRECTIONS** Write a sentence using each word.

gestures     pleading     interfere

_____

_____

_____

_____

**Write in Response to Reading**

Reread from "He picks up on the fourth ring" on p. 164 to "He says good-bye and hangs up" on p. 168. Write an explanatory paragraph using text evidence from the passage to answer the following question: What does the phone call between Hank and Ben reveal about Ben's character? Write your answer below, on a separate sheet of paper, or in a new document.

_____

_____

_____

_____

_____

Students demonstrate contextual understanding of Benchmark Vocabulary. Students read text closely and use text evidence in their written answers.

**Write Dialogue** Write 1–2 pages of dialogue between two characters to add to your narrative. Create a natural dialogue that helps develop your character, and be sure to use concrete words and phrases. Use a separate sheet of paper or start a new document.

**Conventions**

### Indefinite Pronouns

**DIRECTIONS** Underline the indefinite pronoun in the sentence, and write whether it is singular or plural.

1. More were counted this year than last year. _____

2. Most of the water had dried up. _____

3. Somebody must answer the telephone. _____

4. Few have kept the resolutions they made at the beginning of the year.

   _____

5. Some of the children have studied for the test. _____

Students write routinely for a range of tasks, purposes, and audiences. Students practice various conventions of standard English.

**DIRECTIONS** Write a sentence using each word.

lurches        clenches        trudges

_____

_____

_____

_____

**Write in Response to Reading**

Reread the last paragraph on p. 185 through the second paragraph on p. 187. Why did Agatha get involved? Do you think Agatha did the right thing? Write a paragraph using evidence from the text to support your opinion. Use linking words and phrases to show your reasoning. Write your answer below, on a separate sheet of paper, or in a new document.

_____

_____

_____

_____

_____

Students demonstrate contextual understanding of Benchmark Vocabulary. Students read text closely and use text evidence in their written answers.

## Theme

**DIRECTIONS** Using evidence from the text, answer the following questions about Chapter 16 from *Night of the Spadefoot Toads*.

1. What challenges does Ben face in Chapter 16?

   _____

   _____

2. What do we learn about Ben based on his responses to challenges?

   _____

   _____

3. How has Ben changed over the course of the novel?

   _____

   _____

4. Identify two passages in Chapter 16 that relate to the topic of *change over time*.

   _____

   _____

   _____

5. Have any of the other characters in the book changed over time? What caused the change?

   _____

   _____

6. Based on your responses to the previous questions, write one theme present in *Night of the Spadefoot Toads*.

   _____

   _____

Students analyze and respond to literary and informational text.

## Lesson 9

Name _____

**Develop Theme and Resolution** Review your writing products from Lessons 4–8, and use them to write a story that reflects the theme *depending on one another to overcome a challenge*. Your story should include characters, dialogue, a detailed setting, a sequence of events, a conflict, and a resolution. Use a separate sheet of paper or start a new document.

Conventions

## Pronoun-Antecedent Agreement

**DIRECTIONS** Complete each sentence with a pronoun that agrees with the underlined antecedent.

1. <u>Mary</u> played with _____ toys.

2. <u>Frankie</u> bragged to _____ friends.

3. <u>Jenny and I</u> missed _____ school bus.

4. <u>The dog</u> barked, and then _____ ran to catch the ball.

5. <u>The employees</u> received _____ annual evaluations.

 Students write routinely for a range of tasks, purposes, and audiences. Students practice various conventions of standard English.

Name _____

**DIRECTIONS** Write a sentence using each word.

treading    exasperated    skitter

_____

_____

_____

_____

**Write in Response to Reading**

Reread pp. 204–205 of *Night of the Spadefoot Toads*. Write a narrative paragraph that recounts the scene at the vernal pool from Ryan's or Jenny's perspective. Begin by clearly establishing the situation and characters. Include key ideas and important descriptive details. Write your answer below, on a separate sheet of paper, or in a new document.

_____

_____

_____

_____

_____

_____

Students demonstrate contextual understanding of Benchmark Vocabulary. Students read text closely and use text evidence in their written answers.

**Develop Central Conflict or Problem in a Scene** Write a new scene that contains original characters in one setting. Develop a central conflict or problem for the characters. Be sure to include descriptions with sensory details, figurative language, and precise language. Use a separate sheet of paper or start a new document.

**Conventions**

## Agreement with Indefinite Pronouns

**DIRECTIONS** Complete each sentence with the correct pronoun or pronouns.

1. The teacher asked everyone to bring _____ homework the next day.

2. Both work really hard to finish _____ assignments in class.

3. No one should leave _____ belongings unattended.

4. Some of the flowers had lost _____ color.

5. Many will attend the game and bring _____ children along.

 Students write routinely for a range of tasks, purposes, and audiences. Students practice various conventions of standard English.

Name _____

## Compound Words

**DIRECTIONS** Choose the word from the Word Bank that best completes each sentence. Write the word on the line.

### Word Bank

| | | | | |
|---|---|---|---|---|
| postcard | yardstick | blindfold | crybaby | overjoyed |
| waterproof | fourfold | scrapbook | barefoot | greenhouse |
| pinhole | homesick | rowboat | downspout | backpacking |

1. Rain ran from the roof to the ground through a gurgling _____.

2. Susie was very _____ for her friends and her own bed.

3. Through the window, she watched someone fish from a _____.

4. She could put on her _____ poncho and walk to the lake.

5. Instead, she decided to paste pictures into her _____.

6. Meanwhile, Dave was running _____ through the puddles.

7. He carried a _____ he had just picked up from the mailroom.

8. He knew his sister would be _____ to read it.

9. "You can stop being a _____!" he shouted as he came in.

10. "Mom and Dad are on their way back from _____!"

**DIRECTIONS** From the Word Bank, choose the word that best matches each definition. Write the word on the line.

11. a structure for growing plants _____

12. a measuring tool equal to three feet _____

13. four times as much as the original _____

14. a cloth used to cover the eyes _____

15. a very small opening _____

 Students apply grade-level phonics and word analysis skills.

Name _____

**DIRECTIONS** Write a sentence using each word.

wheedle     undergrowth

_____

_____

_____

_____

**Write in Response to Reading**

How has Ben changed during this story? Reread the paragraph on p. 217 that starts with "Without a word, like they speak the same silent language." Use text evidence from the passage and earlier in the story to write an explanatory paragraph. Write your answer below, on a separate sheet of paper, or in a new document.

_____

_____

_____

_____

_____

Students demonstrate contextual understanding of Benchmark Vocabulary. Students read text closely and use text evidence in their written answers.

**Revise a Scene** Review your scene from Lesson 10 and, using your notes from the partner activity, revise your writing to create your desired pace. Remember that the use of dialogue, description, sentence structure, and sentence length all increase interest. Use a separate sheet of paper or start a new document.

**Conventions**

## Action Verbs

**DIRECTIONS** Underline the action verb(s) in each sentence.

1. Mrs. Tibbets watched the snake slither through the leaves.

2. Ben walked along the dirt path and felt happy to be outdoors.

3. Although Ryan is afraid of heights, he hiked up the mountain with his friends.

4. I flew to Texas to visit my grandmother last summer.

5. Caroline feels anxious every time she speaks in front of a large group of people.

Students write routinely for a range of tasks, purposes, and audiences. Students practice various conventions of standard English.

Name _____

**DIRECTIONS** Write a sentence using each word.

fiercely     prejudiced

_____

_____

_____

_____

**Write in Response to Reading**

Reread the dialogue on pp. 4–5, ending with "'Michael!' yelled Esther." Write a short dialogue between Aunt Esther and Michael in which you show a different way that each character might respond to the situation. If possible, use repetition to reveal information about each character. Write your answer on a separate sheet of paper or in a new document.

_____

_____

_____

_____

_____

_____

Students demonstrate contextual understanding of Benchmark Vocabulary. Students read text closely and use text evidence in their written answers.

## Repetition

**DIRECTIONS** Reread the paragraph that begins "Esther liked living alone" on p. 5 of "Shells." Use evidence from the text to answer the following questions.

1. What words and phrases are repeated in this paragraph?

   _____

2. What descriptive details follow each repeated phrase?

   _____

   _____

   _____

3. Which character do these phrases and details describe?

   _____

4. What do these phrases and details suggest about the character?

   _____

   _____

   _____

5. Why do you think the author chose to include these phrases and details?

   _____

   _____

   _____

   _____

Students analyze and respond to literary and informational text.

**Planning a Narrative**  Use a Story Sequence B graphic organizer to plan an original short story. Think about your purpose (to entertain) and your audience (other students) as you complete the graphic organizer. Consider and develop characters and their relationships and interactions, where and when the story takes place, and the sequence of events, including a conflict. Use a separate sheet of paper or start a new document.

**Conventions**

### Use Linking Verbs

**DIRECTIONS**  Underline the linking verb in each sentence. Draw a box around the subject in each sentence, and circle the word that describes the subject.

1. Aunt Esther seemed interested in finding a companion for Sluggo.

2. Michael was surprised by his aunt's sudden interest in his pet.

3. Francine often feels nervous around strangers.

4. Nicholas and his brother are mischievous.

5. Elise is tired of walking to school every day.

Students write routinely for a range of tasks, purposes, and audiences. Students practice various conventions of standard English.

Name _____

**DIRECTIONS** Write a sentence using each word.

assured     craned     stupor

_____

_____

_____

_____

**Write in Response to Reading**

Do you think Michael still hates Aunt Esther? Reread the text on p. 10 that begins with "Oh, what would your mother think, Michael," and ends with "I don't hate you." Organize your ideas logically in a paragraph, and use text evidence from the passage and earlier in the story to support your opinion. Write your answer below, on a separate sheet of paper, or in a new document.

_____

_____

_____

_____

_____

_____

Students demonstrate contextual understanding of Benchmark Vocabulary. Students read text closely and use text evidence in their written answers.

## Welcome to the Neighborhood?

Today more and more people live in homes built where wildlife once roamed freely. Some folks enjoy their animal neighbors. For example, they like watching deer or birds in their backyard. Others view the animals as intruders—unwelcome and annoying. Either way, the fact is that humans are increasingly moving into animal territory. Because interactions between people and wild animals can't be completely avoided, humans must be willing to change some of their habits.

Take birds, for example. They're often attracted to the brilliant lights of city skyscrapers, but the lights can disrupt the birds' migration patterns. Some become exhausted and confused, repeatedly circling the buildings. As a result, the birds fall behind schedule. This increases the likelihood that they won't survive winter storms before reaching their destination. Some cities, such as Chicago, have started voluntary Lights Out programs. Buildings dim or turn off their lights between 11 p.m. and sunrise during the migration season.

Lights on beaches affect wildlife too. Newly hatched sea turtles wait below the sand until dark. Then, instinct and the brightness of the horizon over the water lead them to the sea. If they see lights on the beach, the hatchlings may move toward them and away from the water. They can become dehydrated on land, and car traffic can also endanger them. One solution is to dim or turn the lights off during the periods in which turtle eggs hatch. Another is to direct the light straight down.

Deer, opossums, and raccoons can do serious damage to gardens and homes. Deer will eat a wide variety of plants, but a fence or bright, motion-activated lights may keep them away. By trimming tree branches, homeowners can prevent opossums and raccoons from jumping onto a roof and, from there, entering an attic or a chimney. An effective way to discourage raccoons, as well as coyotes and red foxes, is to keep garbage cans tightly closed. Also, people shouldn't leave food outside for their pets. It may attract wildlife. Even an open bird feeder may attract more than birds.

Some people support trapping and relocating unwanted animals, but these actions are often ineffective. Studies show that more than half of the animals that are relocated won't survive in a new place. Nobody says it will always be easy, but learning how to live side by side with wild animals might be a better solution.

Students read text closely to determine what the text says.

Name _____

**Gather Evidence**  Circle one problem that humans can cause for wildlife, and underline one problem that wildlife can cause for humans. Write a solution to each problem below.

_____

_____

**Gather Evidence: Extend Your Ideas**  Briefly explain how each solution identified solves the problem.

_____

_____

**Ask Questions**  Reread the second paragraph of the article. Write one question you have about bird migration or the Lights Out program. Include at least one detail from the text in your question.

_____

_____

**Ask Questions: Extend Your Ideas**  List two examples of reliable resources you could use to find the answer. Then identify another piece of information on the topic that the resource might include.

_____

_____

**Make Your Case**  Bracket sentences that contain details about the author's point of view on humans and animals living side by side. Then write a sentence describing the author's point of view.

_____

_____

**Make Your Case: Extend Your Ideas**  What is your viewpoint on humans and wildlife sharing the same environment? Discuss this viewpoint with a partner, and use details to support your response.

_____

_____

 Students read text closely to determine what the text says.

Name _____

**Draft a Scene in a Narrative**  Draft one or more of the "events" you planned using the Story Sequence B graphic organizer in Lesson 12. Your scene should help introduce or develop your characters, be part of a larger sequence of events, use transitions to show time and place, and use dialogue and description to develop the scene and characters. Use a separate sheet of paper or start a new document.

**Conventions**

## Use Linking Verbs

**DIRECTIONS**  Underline the verb in each sentence. Above each verb, write A if the verb is used as an action verb or L if the verb is used as a linking verb.

1. The hermit crab grew accustomed to its new home.

2. The hermit crab grew into its new shell.

3. Gerald tasted the ice cream.

4. The ice cream tastes sweet and salty.

5. Maureen looks tired.

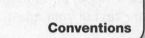

Students write routinely for a range of tasks, purposes, and audiences. Students practice various conventions of standard English.

Name _____

**DIRECTIONS** Write a sentence using each word.

biomes     extinct     dwindled

_____

_____

_____

_____

**Write in Response to Reading**

Choose one of the themes found in *Night of the Spadefoot Toads* and "Shells." Then write an informative paragraph that explains how you know that this theme appears in both texts. Include key details from the texts about Mrs. Tibbets and Aunt Esther to support your explanation. Write your answer below, on a separate sheet of paper, or in a new document.

_____

_____

_____

_____

_____

_____

Students demonstrate contextual understanding of Benchmark Vocabulary. Students read text closely and use text evidence in their written answers.

## Compare and Contrast Characters

**DIRECTIONS** Using evidence from the text, answer the following questions about *Night of the Spadefoot Toads* and "Shells."

1. How are Mrs. Tibbets and Aunt Esther similar in their responses to difficult situations?

   _____

   _____

   _____

2. How are Mrs. Tibbets and Aunt Esther different in their responses to difficult situations?

   _____

   _____

   _____

3. What lesson might a reader learn from Mrs. Tibbets's and Aunt Esther's responses to difficult situations? Use text evidence to explain your answer.

   _____

   _____

   _____

   _____

   _____

   _____

   _____

   _____

Students analyze and respond to literary and informational text.

**Revise or Rewrite a Narrative**  Review another student's narrative draft. On a separate sheet of paper, answer the questions below and suggest improvements.

1. Do transitions clearly indicate sequence?

2. Where could the writer add sensory details?

3. Which verbs could be replaced to be more precise?

4. Does the dialogue sound natural?

5. Is the sentence structure varied?

On a separate sheet of paper or in a new document, revise your narrative using your partner's feedback.

**Conventions**

## Use Verb Phrases

**DIRECTIONS**  Complete each sentence with a verb phrase that uses the verb in parentheses.

1. Ben _____ (help) Mrs. Tibbets in the classroom.

2. Michael _____ (talk) to Aunt Esther about Sluggo.

3. Raquel _____ (go) to ballet practice yesterday.

4. The Johnsons _____ (buy) a new house.

5. We _____ (take) the bus to the museum.

Students write routinely for a range of tasks, purposes, and audiences. Students practice various conventions of standard English.

Name _____

**DIRECTIONS** Write a sentence using each word.

wilderness　　　gingerly　　　survival

_____

_____

_____

_____

**Write in Response to Reading**

Write a brief scene in which Brian responds in a different way to the situation of being injured by the porcupine. Include in your narrative specific details about Brian's traits, feelings, thoughts, and actions based on how he is described in the text. Write your answer on a separate sheet of paper or in a new document.

_____

_____

_____

_____

_____

 Students demonstrate contextual understanding of Benchmark Vocabulary. Students read text closely and use text evidence in their written answers.

**Edit and Proofread a Narrative** Review the revised draft of a new partner, checking for correct grammar and punctuation. Answer the questions below, and write any notes on a separate sheet of paper or in a new document.

1. Are all proper nouns capitalized?

2. Is all dialogue correctly punctuated?

3. Are all words spelled correctly?

When you finish your review, discuss your edits with your partner.

**Conventions**

### Linking Verb or Helping Verb

**DIRECTIONS** Underline the forms of *to be* that are used as linking verbs, and circle the forms of *to be* that are used as helping verbs.

1. Brian is aware that he is crying out of self-pity.

2. We are reading his story, and I am fascinated.

3. Francine was riding her bike yesterday, and she was amazed by how quickly she arrived at her destination.

4. Xavier is studious, but he is having trouble focusing on his work today.

5. My parents were driving to the store on the corner because they were tired.

Students write routinely for a range of tasks, purposes, and audiences. Students practice various conventions of standard English.

## Shades of Meaning

**DIRECTIONS** Read each sentence, and then underline the word in parentheses that best fits the context. Use a dictionary to check meanings if you wish.

1. He (begged, whined) to go to his best friend's play.

2. The losers were (relieved, content) that the game was finally over.

3. Rock climbing can be a (puzzling, challenging) sport.

4. The opponents (debated, questioned) the issues.

5. (Blossoming, Promising) plants can cheer people up in the winter.

6. I admire (artful, crafty) dollhouse rooms.

7. Have you finally (found, recovered) your good health?

8. Let's have less discussion and more (action, achievement)!

9. The triplets are (interchangeable, indistinguishable).

10. We had the (loveliest, prettiest) time on vacation.

**DIRECTIONS** In each line, circle the word that suggests the **strongest** action or feeling.

11. poke        nudge          touch

12. happiness    joy            contentment

13. ability      influence      control

14. guffaw       laugh          giggle

15. bright        dazzling       shiny

**DIRECTIONS** In each line, circle the word that conveys the **weakest** action or feeling.

16. investigate   study          scrutinize

17. mimic         impersonate    copy

18. happen        transpire      befall

19. stumble       trip           lurch

20. anguish       agony          pain

Students apply grade-level phonics and word analysis skills.

Name _____

**DIRECTIONS** Write a sentence using each word.

ignite   registered   painstaking   depression   gratified

_____

_____

_____

_____

_____

_____

_____

**Write in Response to Reading**

Think about the two story events that you compared and contrasted. In your opinion, which event had a greater influence on Brian's actions? State and support your opinion in a brief paragraph. Remember to sequence your ideas logically, and include relevant details from the story to support your opinion. Write your response on a separate sheet of paper or in a new document.

_____

_____

_____

_____

_____

Students demonstrate contextual understanding of Benchmark Vocabulary. Students read text closely and use text evidence in their written answers.

**Publish and Present a Narrative** Publish and read aloud your narrative. Before you present your narrative to the class, annotate it to indicate where to adjust rate and expression. When you speak, adjust rate to build suspense and tension, and make sure to properly reflect characters' emotions and moods in dialogue.

**Conventions**

## Form and Use Principle Parts of Regular Verbs

**DIRECTIONS** Write the correct form of each regular verb.

1. He _____ (*whistle,* present tense) to himself as he follows the trail.

2. Ben is _____ (*pace,* present participle) around the kitchen, unable to sit still.

3. Mrs. Tibbets _____ (*hesitate,* past tense) for a minute before speaking.

4. Mr. Tibbets and his sister had _____ (*play,* past participle) in the marshes.

5. I have _____ (*watch,* past participle) this show for eight years.

Students write routinely for a range of tasks, purposes, and audiences. Students practice various conventions of standard English.

**DIRECTIONS** Write a sentence using each word.

inherited        survival

_____

_____

_____

_____

**Write in Response to Reading**

Identify how a setting similarly influences characters in both texts. Then write a blog entry explaining how each main character's actions are influenced by the setting and how he responds as a result. Include text evidence and remember to quote accurately. Write your answer on a separate sheet of paper or in a new document.

_____

_____

_____

_____

_____

Students demonstrate contextual understanding of Benchmark Vocabulary. Students read text closely and use text evidence in their written answers.

Name _____

## Compare and Contrast Setting

**DIRECTIONS** Using evidence from the text, answer the following questions about *Night of the Spadefoot Toads* and *Hatchet*.

1. What is the setting of each text?

   _____

   _____

2. What passage from each text provides descriptive words and phrases about the setting?

   _____

   _____

3. What influence does each setting have on the main character's actions?

   _____

   _____

4. How are the two characters' actions similar?

   _____

   _____

5. How are the two characters' actions dissimilar?

   _____

   _____

Students analyze and respond to literary and informational text.

Name _____

**Research to Explore Theme**  Use print and digital resources to conduct research about a special environment near you. Find at least two sources. For each source, record a quotation, summary, and paraphrased idea. After drafting, revise your notes to make sure your summaries and paraphrases clearly express the authors' ideas and your quotations have quotation marks. Use a separate sheet of paper or start a new document.

**Conventions**

## Form and Use Principle Parts of Irregular Verbs

**DIRECTIONS**  Write the correct form of each irregular verb.

1. As Mr. Lindsey _____ (*drive,* present tense) away, Ben _____ (*stand,* present tense) by the house.

2. Earlier that day, Ben _____ (*take,* past tense) off his jacket and tied it around his waist.

3. Ben did not know what had happened, but he had _____ (*begin,* past participle) to cry.

4. Just before Michelle _____ (*hide,* past tense) in the closet, she had _____ (*make,* past participle) a loud noise.

5. When Felicia _____ (*go,* past tense) to the restroom, Tristan _____ (*put,* past tense) a note in her backpack.

Students write routinely for a range of tasks, purposes, and audiences. Students practice various conventions of standard English.

Name _____

**DIRECTIONS** Write a sentence using each word.

vernal          prejudiced          ignite

_____

_____

_____

_____

**Write in Response to Reading**

Choose one of the themes common to at least two of the texts. Then write a brief scene in which two characters respond to a challenge. Include dialogue and descriptive details about the characters' thoughts and actions that help reveal the theme you chose. Write your answer on a separate sheet of paper or in a new document.

_____

_____

_____

_____

_____

 Students demonstrate contextual understanding of Benchmark Vocabulary. Students read text closely and use text evidence in their written answers.

Name _____

**Research to Explore Theme** Continue researching and taking notes from sources related to a special natural place that shows a commitment to the environment. After you finish taking notes, write a short story using paraphrased research to support the story. Your writing should include appropriate citations for paraphrased ideas and effective transitional phrases or sentences between ideas. Your story should also have a developed character who has a commitment to the environment, along with a setting, a sequence of events, and a conclusion. Use a separate sheet of paper or start a new document.

**Conventions**

## Form and Use Principal Parts of *To Be*

**DIRECTIONS** Write five sentences that use the verb *to be*. Include at least one sentence that uses the verb in the present tense, one sentence that uses the verb in the past tense, and one sentence that uses its past participle.

1. _____

2. _____

3. _____

4. _____

5. _____

Students write routinely for a range of tasks, purposes, and audiences. Students practice various conventions of standard English.

**Unit 1 • Module A • Lesson 18 • 51**

## Inflected Ending *-ing*

**DIRECTIONS** Change each underlined portion of the sentences so that it reports an event rather than a continuous action. Make sure to pay attention to the verb tense—past, present, or future. Write your change on the line.

1. The rooster was crowing when I woke up. _____

2. Hazel is washing the tablecloth in the sink. _____

3. I wonder what the announcer was thinking. _____

4. Silas will be going to his grandmother's next summer. _____

5. Everybody is clapping for an encore. _____

**DIRECTIONS** Verbs with *-ing* can show continuous action. They can also be used as adjectives, as in "a singing bird." Change the verb in each phrase to an adjective ending in *-ing* and write the new phrase on the line. Make sure to spell the adjective correctly.

6. horse that runs _____

7. story in which a reader becomes absorbed _____

8. puppet that is made to dance _____

9. flower that wilts _____

10. weather that threatens _____

11. breakfast that satisfies _____

12. vote that decides _____

13. visitor who charms _____

14. blanket that comforts _____

15. gardener who digs _____

**DIRECTIONS** In each line, circle the correct spelling.

16. writting     writeing     writing

17. decideing     deciding     decidering

18. qualifying     qualifiing     qualiffying

19. admitting     admiting     admetting

20. judgeing     juddging     judging

Students apply grade-level phonics and word analysis skills.

Name _____

**DIRECTIONS** Write a sentence using each word.

reality     civilization     vied     ultimate

_____

_____

_____

_____

_____

_____

**Write in Response to Reading**

Describe the relationship between Shen and his sister Mei. Use evidence from the text to support your answer. Write your answer below, on a separate sheet of paper, or in a new document.

_____

_____

_____

_____

_____

_____

Students demonstrate contextual understanding of Benchmark Vocabulary. Students read text closely and use text evidence in their written answers.

**Choose and Introduce a Topic**  Write an introductory paragraph for an informative essay about something related to an island environment. Keep in mind that you will use this paragraph and others to develop an essay in Lessons 2–8.

## Form and Use Simple Verb Tenses for Regular Verbs

**DIRECTIONS**  Complete each sentence with the correct form of the verb.

1. I _____ (*play*, present tense) tennis against Alex Chung.

2. Last week, I _____ (*play*, past tense) checkers with Max.

3. Tomorrow, my sister _____ (*drive*, future tense) to New York.

4. We _____ (*walk*, past tense) our dog at the park last weekend.

5. My dad _____ (*cook*, future tense) chili for dinner this Saturday.

Students write routinely for a range of tasks, purposes, and audiences. Students practice various conventions of standard English.

Name _____

**DIRECTIONS** Write a sentence using each word.

shelter    rations

_____

_____

_____

_____

**Write in Response to Reading**

Write a paragraph about being in the rain forest from Mrs. Walpole's point of view. Use details from the text in your paragraph. Write your answer below, on a separate sheet of paper, or in a new document.

_____

_____

_____

_____

_____

_____

Students demonstrate contextual understanding of Benchmark Vocabulary. Students read text closely and use text evidence in their written answers.

Name _____

## Interactions Between Characters and Settings

**DIRECTIONS** Using evidence from the text, answer the following questions about pp. 12–17 of *Washed Up!*

1. What does the reader learn about Gabriela from her actions in the swamp?

   _____

   _____

   _____

2. What does the reader learn about Mei and Shen from their actions on the mountain?

   _____

   _____

   _____

3. What does the reader learn about Oliver from his actions in the rain forest?

   _____

   _____

   _____

4. What does the reader learn about Mrs. Walpole from her actions in the rain forest?

   _____

   _____

   _____

Students analyze and respond to literary and informational text.

**Organize Ideas** Using the introduction that you wrote in Lesson 1, develop an outline for an informative essay on your topic. Use a separate sheet of paper or start a new document.

**Conventions**

## Form and Use Simple Verb Tenses for Irregular Verbs

**DIRECTIONS** Write a sentence using each irregular verb in the tense identified.

1. *write* (past tense)

   _____

2. *ride* (future tense)

   _____

3. *build* (present tense)

   _____

4. *take* (past tense)

   _____

5. *send* (future tense)

   _____

Students write routinely for a range of tasks, purposes, and audiences. Students practice various conventions of standard English.

**DIRECTIONS** Write a sentence using each word.

predicted          teeming

_____

_____

_____

**Write in Response to Reading**

Reread pp. 22–23. Explain how the author's word choice in describing Mr. Garcia and his actions helps develop his character. Write your answer below, on a separate sheet of paper, or in a new document.

_____

_____

_____

_____

 Students demonstrate contextual understanding of Benchmark Vocabulary. Students read text closely and use text evidence in their written answers.

## The BIG Move

Ever since Hannah was an infant, she and her parents had left their tiny city apartment and spent two weeks in the country every June. They rented a big old farmhouse on a large farm. Though the farm was no longer in use, there were acres of fields and woods to explore and even a pond for swimming. Hannah considered those two weeks at the farm the best two weeks of the year.

This June, like every other, everyone packed swimsuits, shorts, and hiking shoes and eagerly headed to the country. Hannah could tell something was different, though, because her mom and dad grew especially quiet as they approached the farm. Hannah figured out why when she saw the big FOR SALE sign posted at the end of the gravel driveway. "The owners are selling the farm! What will we do next June?" Hannah exclaimed.

"How would you feel about living in the farmhouse all year?" Hannah's dad asked. At first, Hannah thought to herself that it sounded fantastic, but then she wasn't so sure. She had lots of questions: *How could she make new friends in the country? Where would she go to school? What do people do for fun in the winter? Could she keep taking karate lessons like she did in the city?*

Hannah's parents tried to reassure her. She would adapt quickly, they explained. Hannah could have friends visit from the city, and she would certainly be able to keep studying karate. Her parents told her they would move before the school year began so that Hannah would have an easier time adjusting. By the end of the week, the decision was finalized. For the next two months, Hannah tried to stay positive. But she also made herself a list of all the things she would miss about city life—like the bright lights at night and all the stores, restaurants, and museums.

When moving day came, Hannah was both excited and nervous—just like her parents. During the first week of school, she made a new friend. Soon the girls started riding their bikes together, and they registered for the same karate class. Hannah even started to enjoy the quietness of the country. It certainly was not as exciting and busy as the city, but the farm was lovely, and the woods were filled with adventures. She could still visit the bright lights and excitement of the big city. Best of all, living in the country versus a small, cramped apartment in the city gave her the best opportunity of all—her family adopted a puppy!

Students read text closely to determine what the text says.

**Gather Evidence**  On p. 59, circle three elements of city life, and underline three elements of country life.

**Gather Evidence: Extend Your Ideas**  Why did Hannah list the things she would miss about city life? Work with a partner and discuss how this list adds to the story.

_____

_____

**Ask Questions**  Draw a box around the questions Hannah asks herself when she learns about her move from the city to the country. Then bracket details in the text that answer some of these questions.

**Ask Questions: Extend Your Ideas**  List three questions that Hannah's parents might have about moving to the country. Do they have anything in common? Explain.

_____

_____

_____

_____

_____

**Make Your Case**  Highlight text that shows Hannah's attitude after the big move. Use these details to write a sentence that includes Hannah's original feelings and how they changed.

_____

_____

**Make Your Case: Extend Your Ideas**  What is your viewpoint on the topic of living in the city versus living in the country? Discuss this viewpoint with a partner.

_____

_____

Students read text closely to determine what the text says.

**Use Quotations to Develop a Topic**  Revise the body paragraphs of your informative essay by including quotations. Find 1–2 quotations that relate to your topic. Incorporate the quotations into your draft, using transitions and your own explanations to show how the quotations support your point. Use correct punctuation to set off the quotations, and include the author's last name and page number in parentheses after the quotation marks. Use a separate sheet of paper or start a new document.

**Conventions**

## Form and Use Perfect Tenses

**DIRECTIONS**  Complete each sentence with the appropriate perfect tense of the verb in parentheses.

1. Amy _____ (*wait*, future perfect) several weeks before reading her reviews.

2. Amy's audience _____ (*read*, past perfect) her book closely, so they had a lot of questions.

3. Amy _____ (*hope*, present perfect) for a best seller for years.

4. Amy _____ (*plan*, past perfect) to complete her new book a month earlier.

5. Amy _____ (*sign*, present perfect) many books for her fans.

Students write routinely for a range of tasks, purposes, and audiences. Students practice various conventions of standard English.

Name _____

**DIRECTIONS** Write a sentence using each word.

frugally    ingenious    windswept

_____

_____

_____

**Write in Response to Reading**

Reread pp. 24–25. Write a paragraph from Mr. Liu's perspective that describes his response to being on the cold mountain. Use details from the text to develop your paragraph. Write your answer below, on a separate sheet of paper, or in a new document.

_____

_____

_____

_____

Students demonstrate contextual understanding of Benchmark Vocabulary. Students read text closely and use text evidence in their written answers.

## Developing Theme

**DIRECTIONS** Using evidence from the text, answer the following questions about pp. 24–27 from *Washed Up!*

1. How does the cold create more than one challenge for the Liu family?

   _____

   _____

   _____

2. How do Mei and Shen respond to the challenge of finding or creating a warmer shelter?

   _____

   _____

   _____

3. What lesson might a reader learn from Mei and Shen's response to finding or creating a warmer shelter on the cold mountain?

   _____

   _____

4. How does the environment make Shen's plan difficult to carry out? How does Shen respond to this challenge?

   _____

   _____

   _____

5. What lesson might a reader learn from Shen's response to this challenge?

   _____

   _____

Students analyze and respond to literary and informational text.

**Develop a Topic with Facts and Details** Continue to develop your informative essay by adding several paragraphs to your draft. Find facts, details, and examples related to how animals, plants, and humans are affected by what is happening in the island environment. Use *Washed Up!* as a guide for which pieces of information to include in your essay, and revise your paragraphs to include these facts, details, and examples. Then revise your paragraphs to vary your sentence structure and include figurative or descriptive language to create interest. Use a separate sheet of paper or start a new document.

**Conventions**

## Form and Use Perfect Tenses

**DIRECTIONS** Write a sentence using each verb in the tense identified.

1. *work* (past perfect)

   _____

2. *influence* (present perfect)

   _____

3. *earn* (future perfect)

   _____

4. *want* (past perfect)

   _____

5. *complete* (future perfect)

   _____

Students write routinely for a range of tasks, purposes, and audiences. Students practice various conventions of standard English.

## Lesson 5

**Benchmark Vocabulary**

Name _____

**DIRECTIONS** Write a sentence using each word.

yielded        glum

_____

_____

_____

_____

**Write in Response to Reading**

Why does Oliver offer to go to the beach? How have previous events led to his offer? Use evidence from the text to support your answer. Write your answer below, on a separate sheet of paper, or in a new document.

_____

_____

_____

_____

_____

_____

Students demonstrate contextual understanding of Benchmark Vocabulary. Students read text closely and use text evidence in their written answers.

Name _____

**Develop a Topic with Domain-Specific Vocabulary** On a separate sheet of paper or in a new document, revise your draft from the previous lesson to include the following:

1. Accurate, precise language instead of language that is too general or vague

2. Domain-specific vocabulary that is appropriate to the topic

3. Definitions and/or explanations that help the reader understand exactly what certain words mean

**Conventions**

## Verb Sequences

**DIRECTIONS** Fill in each blank with the appropriate tense of the verb in parentheses.

Rachel _____ (*crash*) her bicycle last month and _____ (*fracture*) her wrist. Now, she _____ (*wear*) a cast on it, and it _____ (*itch*) a lot. Next month, she _____ (*go*) to the doctor, and he _____ (*remove*) the cast.

 Students write routinely for a range of tasks, purposes, and audiences. Students practice various conventions of standard English.

Name _____

## Homographs and Homonyms

**DIRECTIONS** Read each sentence. The words in parentheses are **homographs**, because they have different pronunciations and meanings. Use context and, if you wish, a dictionary to determine the meanings. On the line, write the definition of the word that makes sense in the sentence.

1. When the low-ranked swimmer won, it was a big (upset, upset)!

   _____

2. The gracious loser seemed to be (content, content) with second place.

   _____

3. She is a (suspect, suspect).

   _____

4. The rope had become (wound, wound) tightly around the pole.

   _____

5. It is hard to understand the (object, object) of this game.

   _____

**DIRECTIONS** Read each sentence. The words in parentheses are **homonyms**, because they have the same pronunciation but different meanings. Use context and, if you wish, a dictionary to determine the meanings. On the line, write the definition of the word that makes sense in the sentence.

6. Can you (bear, bear) to wait another hour for the parade to start?

   _____

7. Although the seats in the front row were (fine, fine), we hung back.

   _____

8. Nothing can (match, match) reading as a great leisure activity.

   _____

9. He prefers the (rose, rose) to the petunia.

   _____

10. Once she drank some of the water, she was able to speak (well, well).

   _____

Students apply grade-level phonics and word analysis skills.

Name _____

**DIRECTIONS** Write a sentence using each word.

murky     squelchy     comfort zones

_____

_____

_____

_____

**Write in Response to Reading**

Reread pp. 35–36. Rewrite the last two paragraphs on p. 36 to include Gabriela's thoughts about wandering off alone and encountering a stranger. Write your paragraphs on a separate sheet of paper or in a new document.

_____

_____

_____

_____

_____

_____

Students demonstrate contextual understanding of Benchmark Vocabulary. Students read text closely and use text evidence in their written answers.

**Develop a Topic with Visuals** On a separate sheet of paper or in a new document, continue to develop your informative essay by adding text features and visuals.

1. Add formatting, such as bold-faced or italicized words and section heads, to clarify organization and emphasize key ideas.

2. Research and add relevant visuals to emphasize and clarify information.

3. Include original captions and labels for photographs, maps, and/or illustrations so that it is clear how the visuals support your essay and add to the topic.

**Conventions**

## Use Verb Sequences

**DIRECTIONS** Complete each sentence with the correct form of the verb.

1. I think Natalie _____ (*join*, past tense) the chorus when she was a freshman.

2. Before she decided to join the chorus, she _____ (*play*, past perfect tense) the saxophone in the band.

3. The chorus instructor believes her singing _____ (*improve*, future tense) if she practices a lot.

4. She has a sore throat because she _____ (*sing*, present perfect tense) the song at least a dozen times.

5. She _____ (*continue*, future tense) to sing when she goes to college.

Students write routinely for a range of tasks, purposes, and audiences. Students practice various conventions of standard English.

Name _____

**DIRECTIONS** Write a sentence using each word.

conclusions          precisely

_____

_____

_____

_____

**Write in Response to Reading**

How does Gabriela's attitude toward Oliver change in Chapter 4? Why do you think her attitude changes? Use text evidence to support your opinion. Write your answer below, on a separate sheet of paper, or in a new document.

_____

_____

_____

_____

_____

Students demonstrate contextual understanding of Benchmark Vocabulary. Students read text closely and use text evidence in their written answers.

## Developing Theme

**DIRECTIONS** Using evidence from the text, answer the following questions about Chapter 4 of *Washed Up!*

1. How does Gabriela first respond to Oliver? Why does she respond this way?

   _____

   _____

   _____

2. Why is it important that Oliver shows Gabriela that there is a hole cut in the fence?

   _____

   _____

   _____

3. What else does Oliver do that helps change Gabriela's attitude toward him? How does Gabriela change?

   _____

   _____

   _____

4. What happens when Gabriela and Oliver meet Shen?

   _____

   _____

5. How do these events help develop a theme?

   _____

   _____

   _____

   _____

Students analyze and respond to literary and informational text.

**Use Transitions to Link Information** On a separate sheet of paper or in a new document, revise your informative essay from the previous lessons. Make sure the organization is easy to identify and the relationships between ideas in and across body paragraphs are clear to the reader. Use cause-effect, chronological, compare-contrast, or sequence transitions to link ideas in your essay.

**Conventions**

## Use Verb Sequences

**DIRECTIONS** Write sentences that include at least two verbs and use the verb tenses identified.

1. Past Perfect: _____

_____

2. Future Perfect: _____

_____

3. Past: _____

_____

4. Present Perfect: _____

_____

5. Future: _____

_____

 Students write routinely for a range of tasks, purposes, and audiences. Students practice various conventions of standard English.

Name _____

**DIRECTIONS** Write a sentence using each word.

notoriously        gratefully        dramatically

_____

_____

_____

_____

**Write in Response to Reading**

Why do you think the Garcias choose to share their prize at the end of the story? Use evidence from the text to support your opinion. Write your answer below, on a separate sheet of paper, or in a new word document.

_____

_____

_____

_____

_____

_____

Students demonstrate contextual understanding of Benchmark Vocabulary. Students read text closely and use text evidence in their written answers.

**Develop a Conclusion** On a separate sheet of paper or in a new document, complete your draft by developing a strong conclusion that brings together (synthesizes) the main ideas of your essay.

**Conventions**

## Use Modal Auxiliary Verbs

**DIRECTIONS** Underline each verb phrase, and circle the modal auxiliary verb.

1. Her fame can give Rachel access to more science information. She should read the latest study on sea lions.

2. She might not have another opportunity like this in a long time. Rachel should take advantage of it.

3. Rachel must finish her latest article for the magazine. She might miss the deadline!

4. She can work late tonight, but her boss says she may have an extra day to work on the article.

 Students write routinely for a range of tasks, purposes, and audiences. Students practice various conventions of standard English.

Name _____

**DIRECTIONS** Write a sentence using each word.

decomposers          organism

_____

_____

_____

_____

**Write in Response to Reading**

Write an opinion paragraph agreeing or disagreeing with the following statement: Organisms within a rain forest food chain are interchangeable. Use definitions and facts from the text to support your reasoning. Include linking words and phrases that show how your ideas and the evidence from the text are related. Write your answer below, on a separate sheet of paper, or in a new document.

_____

_____

_____

_____

_____

_____

Students demonstrate contextual understanding of Benchmark Vocabulary. Students read text closely and use text evidence in their written answers.

Name _____

## Relationships Between Ideas

**DIRECTIONS** Using evidence from the text, answer the following questions about pp. 6–9 from *Rain Forest Food Chains*.

1. How are consumers categorized? What are the three types of consumers?

   _____

   _____

   _____

   _____

2. Review the text and illustration on p. 6. What is the relationship between a primary consumer and a secondary consumer?

   _____

   _____

3. Review the text and illustration on p. 7. How are food chains and food webs related?

   _____

   _____

4. Why is it good for animals to have several food sources?

   _____

   _____

   _____

   _____

5. What purpose do adaptations serve?

   _____

   _____

 Students analyze and respond to literary and informational text.

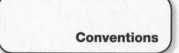
Name _____

**Analyze Text Features and Visuals** Write 1–2 pages analyzing the text features and visuals on pp. 4–11 of *Rain Forest Food Chains*. First, review the text features and visuals, and choose four or five different types that you think are most effective. Then, describe how each text feature or visual organizes or clarifies information for the reader. Finally, write a paragraph about each text feature or visual you have chosen. Use a separate sheet of paper or start a new document.

**Conventions**

## Form and Use Modal Auxiliary Verbs

**DIRECTIONS** Write a sentence using each modal verb below.

**1.** can _____

**2.** could _____

**3.** will _____

**4.** would _____

 Students write routinely for a range of tasks, purposes, and audiences. Students practice various conventions of standard English.

Name _____

**DIRECTIONS** Write a sentence using each word.

producers          relationship

_____

_____

_____

_____

**Write in Response to Reading**

Reread pp. 12–15. Use details from the text to write an informative paragraph explaining the differences between the types of producers found in the rain forest. Write your answer below, on a separate sheet of paper, or in a new document.

_____

_____

_____

_____

_____

_____

Students demonstrate contextual understanding of Benchmark Vocabulary. Students read text closely and use text evidence in their written answers.

Name _____

**Research a Topic** Go on an Internet field trip to reliable sites and find 2–3 text and visual sources about an endangered ecosystem that interests you. Then use the library to find a book on your topic. You will reference these sources in the next lesson. On a separate sheet of paper or in a new document, take one to two pages of notes on your sources, recording key quotations, paraphrases of important ideas, and citation information for each source. Finally, write a paragraph about your experience researching your topic.

Conventions

## Consistency in Verb Tense

**DIRECTIONS** Underline each verb. Cross out any verb tense that is incorrect, and write the correct tense above it.

1. Orchids and bromeliads bring bursts of color to the rain forest. Many orchids had striking, colorful blooms.

2. While Trudy watched a movie in the living room last night, Felix cooks dinner in the kitchen.

3. As the sun set every evening, the sky changes colors.

4. Last week Jonah rides his bike to the museum, but his sister Isabelle took the bus.

5. Movie theaters are crowded on the weekends. People needed something fun to do.

Students write routinely for a range of tasks, purposes, and audiences. Students practice various conventions of standard English.

Name _____

## Words from Spanish

**DIRECTIONS** Write the English word on the line next to the Spanish word that is most like it.

| | | |
|---|---|---|
| _____ | **1.** fabuloso | scorpion |
| _____ | **2.** soledad | market |
| _____ | **3.** acrobata | barbecue |
| _____ | **4.** siesta | minute |
| _____ | **5.** scorpion | perfect |
| _____ | **6.** nevada | acrobat |
| _____ | **7.** mercado | burro |
| _____ | **8.** minuto | siesta |
| _____ | **9.** exquisito | vanilla |
| _____ | **10.** burro | avocado |
| _____ | **11.** perfecto | fabulous |
| _____ | **12.** barbacoa | Nevada |
| _____ | **13.** lazo | solitude |
| _____ | **14.** vainilla | exquisite |
| _____ | **15.** aguacate | lasso |

 Students apply grade-level phonics and word analysis skills.

**DIRECTIONS** Write a sentence using each word.

predators      prey      scavenger

_____

_____

_____

_____

**Write in Response to Reading**

Look at the diagram on p. 24. Use evidence from the text to write and support an opinion statement arguing which link in the food chain—producer, primary consumer, secondary consumer, or decomposer—is most important to the rain forest. Write your answer below, on a separate sheet of paper, or in a new document.

_____

_____

_____

_____

_____

_____

Students demonstrate contextual understanding of Benchmark Vocabulary. Students read text closely and use text evidence in their written answers.

**Synthesize Information from Multiple Sources** Identify 2–3 quotations from either *Washed Up!* or *Rain Forest Food Chains* related to the topic *survival*. Write several paragraphs synthesizing these quotations along with a quotation or paraphrased idea from one of the digital sources you researched in Lesson 10. Be sure to include a Works Cited list for the sources you used. Use a separate sheet of paper or start a new document.

**Conventions**

## Consistency in Verb Tense

**DIRECTIONS** Underline the verbs. Write C if the verb tenses are consistent and I if they are inconsistent. If you write I, change one of the verbs in the sentence to make the tenses consistent. Cross out the verb and write the correct tense above it.

1. Last year, the scientists visit the African rain forest. There, they collected samples of many plant species. _____

2. Next month, the scientists will present their findings to the public. They will explain why protecting the rain forest is important. _____

3. Scientists often discover new species in the rain forest, though most were bugs or fungi. _____

4. In five years, we will buy a new house. It has more space than our condo. _____

5. Many species of plants and animals became extinct because people were not careful. _____

 Students write routinely for a range of tasks, purposes, and audiences. Students practice various conventions of standard English.

Name _____

## Words from French

**DIRECTIONS** Write the English word on the line next to the French word that is most like it.

| | | |
|---|---|---|
| _____ | **1.** etiquette | admit |
| _____ | **2.** disparaitre | beef |
| _____ | **3.** engager | enemy |
| _____ | **4.** lumineux | mathematics |
| _____ | **5.** carre | tablet |
| _____ | **6.** mathematiques | spirit |
| _____ | **7.** boeuf | engage |
| _____ | **8.** admettre | army |
| _____ | **9.** enemi | luminous |
| _____ | **10.** armee | soldier |
| _____ | **11.** tablette | balcony |
| _____ | **12.** esprit | ticket |
| _____ | **13.** raffiner | disappear |
| _____ | **14.** balcon | car |
| _____ | **15.** soldat | refine |

Students apply grade-level phonics and word analysis skills.

Name _____

**DIRECTIONS** Write a sentence using each word.

         dense      practical      native      sustainable

_____

_____

_____

_____

**Write in Response to Reading**

Read the "Kids Can Make a Difference" section on p. 42. Use details from the text to write a paragraph explaining what the children's group does to save their local rain forest. Write your answer below, on a separate sheet of paper, or in a new document.

_____

_____

_____

_____

_____

Students demonstrate contextual understanding of Benchmark Vocabulary. Students read text closely and use text evidence in their written answers.

**Plan an Informative Brochure**  On a separate sheet of paper or in a new document, create an outline for an informative brochure about an ecosystem in jeopardy. Write the name of the ecosystem at the top of your outline. Use Roman numerals to indicate the section headings related to the ecosystem. Below each heading, add key details and terms that you want to include in each section, as well as ideas for effective visuals.

**Conventions**

### Adjectives

**DIRECTIONS**  Circle the adjectives in each sentence. Then underline the noun each adjective modifies.

1. Many colorful butterflies live in the forest.

2. Shaggy, red-haired orangutans are active.

3. The giant anaconda glides through the murky water.

4. Quick monkeys scamper past a sleepy sloth.

5. Long lines of ants carry green bits of leaves to their underground nest.

Students write routinely for a range of tasks, purposes, and audiences. Students practice various conventions of standard English.

Name _____

**DIRECTIONS** Write a sentence using each word.

civilization     predators     sustainable

_____

_____

_____

_____

**Write in Response to Reading**

How do *Rain Forest Food Chains* and *Washed Up!* help you understand the importance of adapting to one's habitat? Use evidence from the texts to support your answer. Write your answer below, on a separate sheet of paper, or in a new document.

_____

_____

_____

_____

_____

Students demonstrate contextual understanding of Benchmark Vocabulary. Students read text closely and use text evidence in their written answers.

Name _____

## The Tree of Heaven

"California, the most wonderful place on the Earth!" sang my father as we trudged through the streets of San Francisco.

I made a face. I had been in California for just a few hours, but already I was terribly homesick for our village in China.

"Here in California," my mother explained to me, "there is wealth everywhere and plenty of jobs to be had."

My father had been to America twice before, without us. He had gotten work in factories and on the railroad. He had saved his earnings. Now our whole family had journeyed across the Pacific to begin our new life in a new land.

"You will like it here, Mei Li," added my mother.

I had lived in our village my whole life—all of ten years. How could I live without our little river, the rice fields, the beautiful Tree of Heaven outside our window? I had not seen a single Tree of Heaven in San Francisco.

"Life is better in America," my father explained as we crossed the dusty street. "China has wars and floods and famines, but such disasters are almost unknown in California."

Perhaps, I thought, but California was crowded, with strange people everywhere, people with too-pale skin and too-light hair, people who jabbered in a language I did not know. The houses looked uninviting, the air smelled different, and how, I wondered, could I ever feel at home here?

"That blue house," said my father, pointing, "is where I lived when I worked in the fish factory seven years ago. It will be our house now that we are immigrants in this land. It can never be the same as our house in China, but we will make it a home."

At first I looked at the house and frowned. Then I noticed something. A tree that I knew well stood outside the blue house. "A Tree of Heaven!" I cried, running to touch the familiar branches.

"A Tree of Heaven at our new home," my father replied. "Seven years ago I took a seed from our Tree of Heaven in China, brought it across the ocean, and planted it here. I know how much you love that tree, Mei Li," he told me, his soft voice quivering. "This house could not be our home without a Tree of Heaven outside."

I breathed in the scent of the leaves, happier than I had been in weeks. "Thank you, Father," I murmured. I walked up to the house and opened the door to our new life.

Students read text closely to determine what
the text says.

**Gather Evidence** Underline text details that reveal Mei Li's opinion of California. Circle text details that reveal her parents' opinions. In the space below, write at least two similarities or differences between Mei Li's opinion and her parents' opinions.

_____

_____

**Gather Evidence: Extend Your Ideas** Review the text details you underlined. What does Mei Li's opinion about California reveal about the character? Discuss your ideas with a partner.

_____

_____

**Ask Questions** Write three questions you have about what happened to Mei Li and her family after the end of the story.

_____

_____

**Ask Questions: Extend Your Ideas** Choose one of the three questions you have about what happened to Mei Li and her family. Scan the text, and bracket any details that might suggest an answer to your question. Then use that bracketed text to write a new question you could ask about the story.

_____

**Make Your Case** Highlight words Mei Li uses to describe California. In a different color, highlight words Mei Li's father uses to describe California. How do these descriptions differ? Write your ideas below.

_____

_____

**Make Your Case: Extend Your Ideas** Does Mei Li begin to feel more positive about her new home by the end of the story? Cite details from the text to support your answer.

_____

_____

 Students read text closely to determine what the text says.

**Draft an Informative Brochure** Draft 2–3 paragraphs of your informative brochure based on the outline you created in Lesson 12, using your section headings to organize the information logically. Be sure to include precise language, descriptive details, and examples. Use a separate sheet of paper or start a new document.

**Conventions**

**Use Adverbs**

**DIRECTIONS** Circle the adverbs. Then underline the word or words each adverb modifies.

1. Rachel carefully removed the seashell and gently brought it to her ear.

2. Then the jaguar moved slowly across the rain forest floor, quietly stalking its prey.

3. The bird flew gracefully above the mountains and landed on a tall tree.

4. Noelle wandered freely around the house, exploring every room she passed.

5. Anthony and Andrea eagerly cleaned their apartment, but they were very tired when they finished.

Students write routinely for a range of tasks, purposes, and audiences. Students practice various conventions of standard English.

Name _____

**DIRECTIONS** Write a sentence using each word.

distinctive     thrived     exclusive     ornate

_____

_____

_____

_____

_____

**Write in Response to Reading**

Write an explanatory paragraph about what Pale Male did to settle in at Central Park. Use specific details and examples of figurative language from the text to support your explanation. Write your answer below, on a separate sheet of paper, or in a new document.

_____

_____

_____

_____

_____

 Students demonstrate contextual understanding of Benchmark Vocabulary. Students read text closely and use text evidence in their written answers.

Name _____

## Sentence Structure and Figurative Language

**DIRECTIONS**  Using evidence from the text, answer the following questions about pp. 29–36 from *Pale Male*.

1.  What does the description of traffic as ant-like on p. 29 help the reader understand?

    _____

    _____

2.  Read the first paragraph on p. 30. How does the sentence structure connect two ideas?

    _____

    _____

    _____

    _____

3.  Read the second paragraph on p. 30. How does the sentence structure help reflect a contrasting idea about Pale Male?

    _____

    _____

    _____

    _____

4.  Read the first two paragraphs on p. 35. What effect does using shorter sentences in the second paragraph have on the text?

    _____

    _____

    _____

5.  Read the final two sentences of the last paragraph on p. 36. What idea does their sentence structure help emphasize?

    _____

    _____

    _____

    _____

Students analyze and respond to literary and informational text.

Name _____

**Revise or Rewrite an Informative Brochure** Work with a partner to peer review the drafts you wrote in Lesson 13. First, make sure the organization makes sense, adding transitions if necessary. Next, look for vague or general language that could be more precise, and replace it with specific language appropriate to the audience. Finally, suggest visuals that would help clarify information or support points. After you complete your peer review, use a separate sheet of paper or a new document to revise or rewrite parts of your own brochure, adding visuals and improving word choice. Refer to *Pale Male* as a guide for precise language and transitions.

**Conventions**

## Predicate Adjectives and Linking Verbs

**DIRECTIONS** Circle the linking verbs and underline the predicate adjectives.

1. The students were upset when they saw that Pigeon Creek was full of litter. They seemed determined to clean up the creek.

2. Nancy looked relaxed as she drank a cup of tea. She felt sleepy a few minutes later.

3. Whenever Jasmine is bored, she goes to the library and looks for a book that seems interesting.

4. Sara could not understand why her mother had become so frustrated so quickly.

5. Aliyah felt sad as she watched her best friend drive away for the last time.

Students write routinely for a range of tasks, purposes, and audiences. Students practice various conventions of standard English.

Name _____

**DIRECTIONS** Write a sentence using each word.

substantial    perseverance    renovate

_____

_____

_____

_____

**Write in Response to Reading**

On pp. 44–45, the author describes what happens after the first of Pale Male's three fledglings attempts to fly. Is this description effective in helping the reader visualize the events? State your opinion, and support it using reasons and evidence from the text. Write your answer below, on a separate sheet of paper, or in a new document.

_____

_____

_____

_____

_____

Students demonstrate contextual understanding of Benchmark Vocabulary. Students read text closely and use text evidence in their written answers.

Name _____

## Cause and Effect

**DIRECTIONS** Using evidence from the text, answer the following questions about pp. 38–42 from *Pale Male*.

1. What caused the removal of the hawks' nest from 927 Fifth Avenue? Cite text evidence in your answer.

_____

_____

_____

_____

2. How did this event affect "the hawks' small fan club"?

_____

_____

3. The hawks rebuilt a nest on the same spot. What were some effects of this new construction?

_____

_____

_____

_____

4. Choose one of these effects and change it to a cause. What is one effect of this new cause?

_____

_____

 Students analyze and respond to literary and informational text.

Name _____

**Edit and Proofread an Informative Brochure**  Edit and proofread the informative brochure you drafted in Lesson 13 and revised in Lesson 14. Check for complete sentences, subject-verb agreement, correct verb forms, and consistent verb tenses. Also check for correct spelling, punctuation, and capitalization. Make your edits on a separate sheet of paper or in a new document.

**Conventions**

### Predicate Adjectives and Linking Verbs

**DIRECTIONS**  Underline the linking verb in each sentence. In the space after the sentence, write the number of predicate adjectives that follow the linking verb.

1. The students were startled and amazed when the eggs started spinning. ____

2. The alevins looked strange with their big orange yolk sacs. ____

3. Even if a wild animal seems harmless, you should approach it carefully. ____

4. The girl became famous after appearing on a talent show. ____

5. The carpenters felt tired and sore after a long day of work. ____

Students write routinely for a range of tasks, purposes, and audiences. Students practice various conventions of standard English.

## Suffixes -*tion*, -*ion*

**DIRECTIONS** Change each verb to a noun by adding the suffix -*tion* or -*ion*. Remember to change the spelling of the base word if necessary when you add the ending. Then write a sentence using the noun on the line.

1. rotate _____

2. act _____

3. permit _____

4. relate _____

5. promote _____

6. graduate _____

7. confuse _____

8. explain _____

9. invite _____

10. revise _____

11. operate _____

12. admit _____

13. attract _____

14. constitute _____

15. complicate _____

 Students apply grade-level phonics and word analysis skills.

Name _____

**DIRECTIONS** Write a sentence using each word.

conservation     protests     relentless

_____

_____

_____

_____

**Write in Response to Reading**

Choose one of the problems Pale Male faced after he arrived in Central Park. Write an informative paragraph describing the problem and the reasons it occurred. Be sure to include specific details and examples from the text. Write your answer below, on a separate sheet of paper, or in a new document.

_____

_____

_____

_____

_____

Students demonstrate contextual understanding of Benchmark Vocabulary. Students read text closely and use text evidence in their written answers.

Name _____

**Publish and Present an Informative Brochure** If available, use publishing software to create a digital version of your brochure. Otherwise, use separate sheets of paper, and cut out photos to create an interesting and informative layout. Enhance your main ideas with photos, graphs, maps, and charts. As part of a classroom "ecotourism conference," present your brochure to inform and promote travel to your ecosystem. Adapt your speaking pace and tone to the audience and subject matter.

## Degrees of Comparison

**DIRECTIONS** In each sentence, underline the adjective or adverb that shows a degree of comparison. On the line that follows, write PD if the word shows a positive degree of comparison, CD if it shows a comparative degree of comparison, or SD if it shows a superlative degree of comparison.

1. The students' plans to keep Pigeon Creek clean worked really well. _____

2. The worst part about the pollution in Pigeon Creek was that it made it impossible for salmon and other living things to survive in it. _____

3. In my opinion, it is more convenient to keep the town park clean than it is to pick up trash that people have left on the ground. _____

4. Volunteering to clean up a park is a good way to contribute positively to your community. _____

5. A better way to reduce litter in your community is to always put trash in a garbage can and encourage your friends and family to do the same. _____

Students write routinely for a range of tasks, purposes, and audiences. Students practice various conventions of standard English.

Name _____

**DIRECTIONS** Write a sentence using each word.

perseverance

_____

_____

_____

_____

**Write in Response to Reading**

Write two paragraphs that analyze the word choice in *Washed Up!* and *Pale Male*. How does the author's use of certain words add meaning in each text? Use evidence from the texts to support your answer. Write your response on a separate sheet of paper or in a new document.

_____

_____

_____

_____

_____

_____

Students demonstrate contextual understanding of Benchmark Vocabulary. Students read text closely and use text evidence in their written answers.

Name _____

**Compare and Contrast Information** Draft an outline for your essay that includes the main idea about the two ecosystems you chose as well as 2–3 similarities and 2–3 differences between them. Use a consistent, logical organization for your outline. To clarify comparisons and contrasts among ideas, use transitions such as *similarly, however,* and *although.*

**Conventions**

## Understand Degrees of Comparison

**DIRECTIONS** Write a sentence using each adjective in the form identified in parentheses.

1. *heavy* (comparative)

_____

2. *smart* (superlative)

_____

3. *hard* (comparative)

_____

4. *good* (superlative)

_____

5. *exciting* (superlative)

_____

 Students write routinely for a range of tasks, purposes, and audiences. Students practice various conventions of standard English.

Name _____

**DIRECTIONS** Write a sentence using each word.

organism          distinctive          conservation

_____

_____

_____

_____

**Write in Response to Reading**

How do *Washed Up!, Rain Forest Food Chains,* and *Pale Male* each address the way organisms (plants or animals) in a particular habitat affect each other? How are they similar or different in their approach? Use examples from the text in your response. Write your response on a separate sheet of paper or in a new document.

_____

_____

_____

_____

_____

Students demonstrate contextual understanding of Benchmark Vocabulary. Students read text closely and use text evidence in their written answers.

## Multiple Accounts

**DIRECTIONS** Using evidence from the text, answer the following questions about *Washed Up!*, *Rain Forest Food Chains*, and *Pale Male*.

1. Which passages in each text address the topic of habitats?

   _____

   _____

   _____

2. How are the passages you identified similar?

   _____

   _____

   _____

3. How are the passages you identified different?

   _____

   _____

   _____

4. Based on the similarities and differences among the texts in addressing the topic of habitats, what conclusions can you draw about each text?

   _____

   _____

   _____

Students analyze and respond to literary and informational text.

**Develop an Opinion Statement** Use the outline you created in Lesson 17 to draft an introduction, body paragraphs, and conclusion for your opinion statement. Your draft should include a clear statement of opinion, facts and evidence to support logically ordered reasons, and a conclusion that summarizes your main points and includes a call to action. Use a separate sheet of paper or start a new document.

Conventions

## Form and Use Irregular Comparisons

**DIRECTIONS** Circle the word in the parentheses that correctly completes the sentence.

1. Driving a car is (badder/worse) for the environment than riding a bike.

2. You can travel (farther/farer) on a bike than you can on foot.

3. It is (gooder/better) to recycle plastic packaging than to discard it with the regular trash, but buying fewer products packaged in plastic is (goodest/best) of all.

4. We can all feel (weller/better) about ourselves if we do our part to protect the environment.

5. "This is the (baddest/worst) hotel I have ever stayed in. Driving across town to stay at another hotel is (gooder/better) than staying here another night!" said Miles.

Students write routinely for a range of tasks, purposes, and audiences. Students practice various conventions of standard English.

## Words from Spanish

**DIRECTIONS** The Word Bank consists of English words that come from Spanish words. Use one or more of these words to complete each sentence. You will use each word just once. If you need to check the definition of a word, use a dictionary.

### Word Bank

| | | | | |
|---|---|---|---|---|
| barbecue | burros | hurricane | tornado | pueblos |
| cargo | arroyos | canyons | chaps | papaya |
| corrals | lariat | ranch | rodeo | tomato |
| adobe | avocado | chilies | mesas | guacamole |

1. We are going to use hot coals to _____ the meat.

2. We will mash _____ and add _____ and onion to make

   some delicious _____.

3. To spice up the meal, we will add some hot _____.

4. We will chop the fruit we call _____ and add it to the plates to help
   people cool their mouths.

5. Today, there is no rain and the _____ are without water.

6. In the distance we see the _____, which look like giant footstools
   made of rock.

7. Beyond those are the deep _____ that were cut by centuries of
   running water.

8. Along their sides, ancient people built _____ out of a material called

   _____.

9. They used _____ to haul _____.

10. At the end of the day, they kept the animals in _____.

11. Sometimes, a cowboy called a *vaquero* has to catch livestock using a rope called a

    _____.

12. With a lot of practice working on the _____, a cowboy can qualify

    to compete in a _____.

13. Competitors wear _____ to protect their legs.

14. Some of the bucking broncos are so athletic that they spin like a

    _____ or a _____.

 Students apply grade-level phonics and word
analysis skills.

Name _____

**DIRECTIONS** Write a sentence using each word.

debts      auction      master

_____

_____

_____

_____

**Write in Response to Reading**

Why do you think the narrator and her mother did not escape immediately after her father was sold? Use text evidence to support your opinion. Write your answer below, on a separate sheet of paper, or in a new document.

_____

_____

_____

_____

_____

Students demonstrate contextual understanding of Benchmark Vocabulary. Students read text closely and use text evidence in their written answers.

Name _____

**Analyze Point of View** Analyze how point of view influences your understanding of the story. Choose a passage from Chapter 1 that shows the narrator's point of view. Consider how the passage would be different if it were told from a different person's point of view. On a separate sheet of paper or in a new document, write 1–2 paragraphs that analyze how the narrator offers an insight on the subject, and use text evidence to express your opinion about how the narrator's point of view influences you.

**Conventions**

## Form and Use Gerunds

**DIRECTIONS** Answer the following questions using gerunds.

1. What are your hobbies?

_____

2. What chores are you responsible for at home?

_____

_____

3. What is something you are good at?

_____

4. What is something you are not good at?

_____

5. What is your favorite activity in PE class?

_____

 Students write routinely for a range of tasks, purposes, and audiences. Students practice various conventions of standard English.

**DIRECTIONS** Write a sentence using each word.

stumble     plantation     patrolled

_____

_____

_____

_____

**Write in Response to Reading**

Compare the large, two-page illustration on pages 12 and 13 to the small illustrations on pages 14 and 15. What sort of things are big illustrations good for? What sort of things are small illustrations good for? Use text evidence to support your answer. Write your answer below, on a separate sheet of paper, or in a new document.

_____

_____

_____

_____

_____

_____

Students demonstrate contextual understanding of Benchmark Vocabulary. Students read text closely and use text evidence in their written answers.

## Illustrations

**DIRECTIONS** Using evidence from the text, answer the following questions about pages 10–16 from *The Road to Freedom*.

1. Look at the illustrations on pages 10–13. What do they show?

   _____

   _____

2. What do these illustrations say about their journey?

   _____

   _____

3. Look at the illustrations on pages 14–16. What do they show?

   _____

   _____

   _____

4. What do these illustrations say about their journey?

   _____

   _____

5. On page 15, Emma tries not to think about their cabin, her pallet, or a fire. Why do you think these details were not included in the illustrations?

   _____

   _____

   _____

 Students analyze and respond to literary and informational text.

**Analyze Visual Elements** Choose illustrations from the text, and write three opinion paragraphs about what they contribute to the text in terms of meaning, tone, and beauty. First, determine which lines of text relate to the illustrations. Then, think about how the visuals emphasize ideas or descriptive details in the text. Finally, consider how the illustrations relate to the text's mood or tone and deepen your overall understanding of the text. Use a separate sheet of paper or start a new document.

**Conventions**

## Participles

**DIRECTIONS** Write a sentence with each participle below.

**1.** boring _____

**2.** frozen _____

**3.** burnt _____

**4.** surprising _____

**5.** tired _____

Students write routinely for a range of tasks, purposes, and audiences. Students practice various conventions of standard English.

Name _____

**DIRECTIONS** Write a sentence using each word.

curled     screech     grumbled

_____

_____

_____

_____

**Write in Response to Reading**

Many writers try to make the reader feel as if he or she is a part of the story. How do the story structure and details used in the text make you feel like you are a part of the story? Support your answer with text evidence. Write your answer below, on a separate sheet of paper, or in a new document.

_____

_____

_____

_____

_____

Students demonstrate contextual understanding of Benchmark Vocabulary. Students read text closely and use text evidence in their written answers.

## The Price of Freedom

What are you worth? If you were enslaved in the United States in 1850, you were a possession. Slave owners could buy and sell you for as much as $3,000. For this reason, slave owners offered rewards for the capture of enslaved people who had escaped.

The Underground Railroad was a secret network of people who believed that slavery was wrong. They risked the consequences of breaking the law to help people escape slavery and make their way to northern states or Canada, where slavery was outlawed. The use of railroad terms helped ensure secrecy. Routes between *stations*—homes of sympathetic families who would feed and hide the enslaved people—were called *lines*. *Conductors* guided runaways from one station to another. Fugitives were referred to as *packages* or *freight*.

Those people who contributed to the Underground Railroad included free African Americans and sympathetic whites. However, one of the best-known conductors had escaped slavery herself. Harriet Tubman was born enslaved in Maryland around 1820. By the fall of 1849, Tubman made the decision to flee. If she couldn't have freedom, she would prefer death. A friendly white neighbor told her how to find the first safe house on her path to freedom. When she finally reached the North, where slavery was outlawed, Harriet said, "I had crossed the line. I was free; but there was no one to welcome me to the land of freedom. I was a stranger in a strange land."

Harriet's goal became to help those she had left behind, including her family members. Rather than simply enjoying her newly found freedom, she got a job in Philadelphia and saved her money. In 1850, Harriet returned to Maryland and started leading her family to freedom. Over the next ten years, she made the hazardous trip south and back numerous times. Because of Harriet's efforts, her family and around seventy other enslaved people escaped slavery. She never "lost" a fugitive. She never allowed anyone to give up. Harriet was so determined to see these people reach freedom that she carried a gun to threaten the fugitives if they became too tired or decided to turn back. When a person's resolve wavered, she advised, "You'll be free or die."

One newspaper in Maryland offered a $100 reward for her capture. But to the scores of people Harriet Tubman helped to reach freedom, she was priceless!

Students read text closely to determine what the text says.

**Gather Evidence** On page 111, underline the text details that explain why Harriet was willing to help enslaved people escape at the risk of her own freedom.

**Gather Evidence: Extend Your Ideas** Review the text details. What do Harriet's actions after she escaped slavery reveal about her? Discuss your ideas with your partner.

_____

_____

_____

**Ask Questions** Write two questions you have about slavery and the Underground Railroad.

_____

_____

**Ask Questions: Extend Your Ideas** Choose one of the two questions you have about slavery and the Underground Railroad. Scan the text on page 111, and circle any details that might suggest an answer to your question. Then use that circled text to write another question.

_____

**Make Your Case** On page 111, circle descriptive details that the author uses to describe the Underground Railroad. Which ones are related? Write them below.

_____

_____

_____

_____

 Students read text closely to determine what the text says.

**Analyze Author's Style** On a separate sheet of paper or in a new document, write three or more paragraphs about the author's style in *The Road to Freedom* based on a five- to ten-line paragraph from the text. Consider factors such as sentence length, interesting or unusual word choices, use of dialect, and use of idiomatic expressions. Explain how these choices demonstrate the author's style. Start the paragraphs by stating your opinion on whether or not the author's style contributes to the meaning of the text.

**Conventions**

## Infinitives

**DIRECTIONS** Write a sentence with each infinitive below.

**1.** to bake _____

**2.** to walk _____

**3.** to look _____

**4.** to collect _____

**5.** to dance _____

 Students write routinely for a range of tasks, purposes, and audiences. Students practice various conventions of standard English.

Name _____

**DIRECTIONS** Write a sentence using each word.

shivering    scent    quilt

_____

_____

_____

_____

**Write in Response to Reading**

Think about how Emma and her mother responded to the storm. How would they have responded if they were not escaped slaves? What other events in the story would they have responded to differently if they were not escaped slaves? Write your answer below, on a separate sheet of paper, or in a new document.

_____

_____

_____

_____

_____

Students demonstrate contextual understanding of Benchmark Vocabulary. Students read text closely and use text evidence in their written answers.

**Develop an Opinion Statement and Introduction**  Choose a topic discussed in *The Road to Freedom,* and consider how the author develops it with details in the text. Then, formulate an opinion about the issue, and state it clearly. Finally, develop an introductory paragraph using this opinion statement. Write your paragraph on a separate sheet of paper or in a new document.

**Conventions**

## Prepositions

**DIRECTIONS**  Write five sentences describing your bedroom using prepositions.

_____

_____

_____

_____

_____

 Students write routinely for a range of tasks, purposes, and audiences. Students practice various conventions of standard English.

Name _____

**DIRECTIONS** Write a sentence using each word.

conductor     slavery     shuffling

_____

_____

_____

_____

**Write in Response to Reading**

Reread the first paragraph on page 28. Why is it called the Underground Railroad even though there are no trains or tracks? Why does the old woman say her house is a station? Write you answer below, on a separate sheet of paper, or in a new document.

_____

_____

_____

_____

_____

Students demonstrate contextual understanding of Benchmark Vocabulary. Students read text closely and use text evidence in their written answers.

## Word Choice

**DIRECTIONS** Using evidence from the text, answer the following questions about pages 27–32 from *The Road to Freedom*.

1. The first sentence of the chapter describes the house as warm. What other words in the first paragraph reinforce this idea?

_____

_____

2. Why do you think the idea of warmth is emphasized?

_____

_____

_____

_____

3. Look at page 29. What words and phrases show a sense of urgency?

_____

4. Look at the word choices used to describe the men who came to the house and their actions. What kind of men are they?

_____

_____

5. Look at the description of the boots on page 32. What do they tell you about the old woman?

_____

_____

_____

_____

_____

Students analyze and respond to literary and informational text.

Name _____

**Gather Evidence to Support an Opinion** Develop your opinion statement from the previous lesson. Review your introductory paragraph, gather supporting evidence (facts, details, quotations, etc.), and use the evidence to develop at least three reasons to support your opinion statement. On a separate sheet of paper or in a new document, write two to three body paragraphs that present your reasons in a logical order.

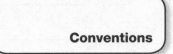

**Conventions**

**Prepositional Phrases**

**DIRECTIONS** Complete each sentence with a prepositional phrase.

1. I like to shop _____.

2. I ate potatoes _____.

3. I received a toy _____.

4. My cat likes to sleep _____.

5. I put syrup _____.

Students write routinely for a range of tasks, purposes, and audiences. Students practice various conventions of standard English.

## Word Families

**DIRECTIONS**  Each web contains a word that is part of a word family. Complete each web with words from the Word Bank. Use a dictionary to check the meanings of the words.

### Word Bank

| | | | | |
|---|---|---|---|---|
| posture | flambé | ringleader | imposition | inflammatory |
| earring | superimpose | inflame | familiar | boring |
| deregulate | juxtapose | ringlet | clearance | flammable |
| daring | clarification | flamboyant | reclassify | ringside |
| clarity | family | imposing | impossible | clearing |

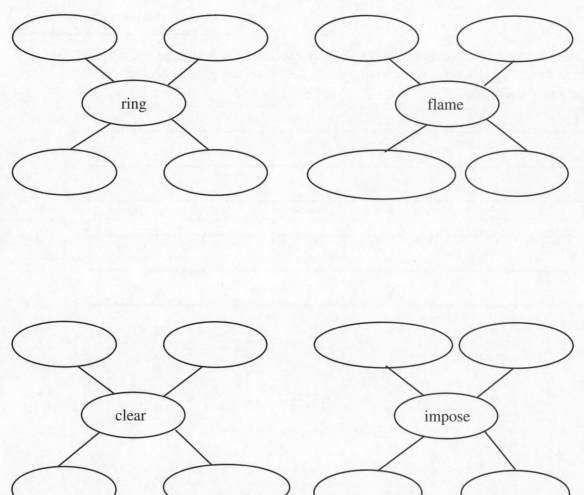

Students apply grade-level phonics and word analysis skills.

Name _____

**DIRECTIONS**  Write a sentence using each word.

tumbled     whinnied     stuttered

_____

_____

_____

_____

**Write in Response to Reading**

Compare this chapter to the previous chapter. Briefly explain what is similar and what is different in these two chapters. Write your answer below, on a separate sheet of paper, or in a new document.

_____

_____

_____

_____

_____

_____

Students demonstrate contextual understanding of Benchmark Vocabulary. Students read text closely and use text evidence in their written answers.

**Organize Ideas** On a separate sheet of paper or in a new document, draft an outline to further develop your opinion paragraphs from the previous lesson. Decide on an organizational structure and sort the information you gathered into an outline. Use the outline to revise and reorganize your body paragraphs, and add transitions to link ideas and clarify organization.

**Conventions**

## Prepositions and Pronouns

**DIRECTIONS** Replace the underlined word(s) with a pronoun in the correct case.

1. Sean played with Felicia and Thomas for hours. _____

2. My sister looked behind Frank and saw his mother approaching. _____

3. I reserved a table for Marissa and me at her favorite restaurant. _____

4. He gave the ball to his brothers and walked away. _____

5. Oh no! Eric is scared of Roxanne! _____

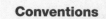

Students write routinely for a range of tasks, purposes, and audiences. Students practice various conventions of standard English.

Name _____

**DIRECTIONS** Write a sentence using each word.

drifted    lantern    scattered

_____

_____

_____

_____

**Write in Response to Reading**

Look at the song lyrics on page 42. If you have heard the song before, describe the tone and how it fits with the story. If you have not heard the song before, what kind of tone would you guess it has? Do you think someone would sing it slowly or quickly? Do you think they would sing it loudly or softly? What emotions does this song convey? Write your answer below, on a separate sheet of paper, or in a new document.

_____

_____

_____

_____

_____

Students demonstrate contextual understanding of Benchmark Vocabulary. Students read text closely and use text evidence in their written answers.

**Strengthen Reasons and Evidence** On a separate sheet of paper or in a new document, revise your opinion essay from Lesson 6. First, find a partner and trade essays. Review your partner's essay, looking for weak reasons and insufficient evidence. Give your suggestions to your partner, and consider his or her suggestions for your own essay. Then revise your essay by deleting any irrelevant evidence; adding relevant evidence, such as facts, precise details, and quotations; and adding transitions where needed to make connections between the evidence and your opinions clear to the reader.

**Conventions**

## Differentiate Prepositions and Adverbs

**DIRECTIONS** For each word, write one sentence using it as an adverb and one sentence using it as a preposition.

1. down:   adverb _____

   preposition _____

   _____

2. inside:   adverb _____

   preposition _____

3. over:   adverb _____

   preposition _____

 Students write routinely for a range of tasks, purposes, and audiences. Students practice various conventions of standard English.

Name _____

**DIRECTIONS** Write a sentence using each word.

hunched    capturing    blisters    carriage

_____

_____

_____

_____

_____

_____

**Write in Response to Reading**

Look at the train on page 50. Compare this train to trains you have ridden in or seen. What do you think it was like to ride on this train? Write your answer below, on a separate sheet of paper, or in a new document.

_____

_____

_____

_____

_____

_____

Students demonstrate contextual understanding of Benchmark Vocabulary. Students read text closely and use text evidence in their written answers.

Name _____

## Information from Illustrations

**DIRECTIONS** Using evidence from the text, answer the following questions about pages 45–50 from *The Road to Freedom*.

1. Look at the illustration on page 45. Is this something that happened on the journey? How do you know?

   _____

   _____

2. What idea from page 46 do the illustrations on page 47 emphasize?

   _____

   _____

3. Look at the illustration on pages 48–49. Which details from the text are depicted in the illustration? What does the illustration help the reader understand about Philadelphia?

   _____

   _____

   _____

   _____

4. What does the image of the train on page 50 help you understand about the next part of Emma and Mama's journey?

   _____

   _____

   _____

Students analyze and respond to literary and informational text.

**Use Transitions to Clarify an Opinion**  Trade essays with a new partner, and review his or her essay. When reviewing your partner's essay, determine the overall structure, and suggest transitions that can clarify the essay's organization and purpose. Then identify the opinion statement, and suggest transitions that connect it to evidence and reasons. Share your suggestions with your partner, and then revise your own essay using his or her feedback. Write you revisions on a separate sheet of paper or in a new document.

**Conventions**

## Use Coordinating Conjunctions

**DIRECTIONS**  Add a conjunction and independent clause to each of the independent clauses below. Be sure to punctuate your sentences correctly.

1. On Friday, we saw a movie _____.

2. He bought some milk at the store _____.

3. _____ you shouldn't eat too much.

4. The plane leaves at 8:00 a.m. _____

5. _____ I love pizza.

Students write routinely for a range of tasks, purposes, and audiences. Students practice various conventions of standard English.

Name _____

**DIRECTIONS** Write a sentence using each word.

surrounded    pillars    territory

_____

_____

_____

_____

**Write in Response to Reading**

What do you think is the most important theme in *The Road to Freedom*? Use evidence from the text to support your opinion. Write your answer below, on a separate sheet of paper, or in a new document.

_____

_____

_____

_____

_____

_____

Students demonstrate contextual
understanding of Benchmark Vocabulary.
Students read text closely and use text
evidence in their written answers.

**Develop a Conclusion** Review your essay, and on a separate sheet of paper or in a new document, write a concluding paragraph for it. Include a brief summary of your main ideas or points, and add at least one new insight, reflection, or "call to action."

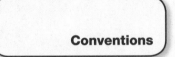

**Conventions**

### Interjections

**DIRECTIONS** Write a sentence that uses an interjection to express each emotion or action below.

1. Happiness: _____

2. Dismay: _____

3. Surprise: _____

4. To attract attention: _____

5. To show concern: _____

 Students write routinely for a range of tasks, purposes, and audiences. Students practice various conventions of standard English.

Name _____

**DIRECTIONS** Write a sentence using each word.

historical     abolish     tremendous

_____

_____

_____

_____

**Write in Response to Reading**

The methods of escape used by Emma and her mother were based on historical accounts. What are some of the methods they used? Can you think of other ways slaves may have escaped? Write your answer below, on a separate sheet of paper, or in a new document.

_____

_____

_____

_____

_____

_____

Students demonstrate contextual understanding of Benchmark Vocabulary. Students read text closely and use text evidence in their written answers.

Name _____

## Compare Historical Accounts

**DIRECTIONS**  Using evidence from the text, answer the following questions about pages 55–56 from *The Road to Freedom*.

1. Reread the last sentence of the first paragraph of the epilogue. Can you think of other examples of secret signals or codes mentioned in previous chapters of the text?

   _____

   _____

   _____

2. Based on the story and the epilogue, what are some of the reasons abolitionists helped slaves escape?

   _____

   _____

   _____

3. Based on details in the story and the epilogue, did this story take place before or after 1850?

   _____

   _____

   _____

   _____

4. The epilogue has more facts than the story. Why do you think this is?

   _____

   _____

   _____

   _____

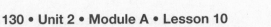
Students analyze and respond to literary and informational text.

**Analyze Multiple Perspectives** Choose an important historical milestone or event described in *The Road to Freedom*. Then write a social media message, about 300 words long, that presents multiple perspectives on how the event impacted people. Consider how the event might have impacted an individual family, people in different areas of the country, and the country as a whole. Support your ideas with text evidence. Use a separate sheet of paper or start a new document.

**Conventions**

## Correlative Conjunctions

**DIRECTIONS** Match the sentence fragments to make complete sentences.

1. When you get to the bus station, either Jared

   **a.** or see a movie.

2. I'm sorry, but neither Kim

   **b.** nor Scott will be there.

3. We can either go shopping

   **c.** nor play golf.

4. The burglars took not only our TV

   **d.** but also some of Mom's jewelry.

5. After I injured my wrist, I could neither bowl

   **e.** or Jacob will pick you up.

Students write routinely for a range of tasks, purposes, and audiences. Students practice various conventions of standard English.

**Endings -s, -ed, -ing**

**DIRECTIONS** Read each sentence. Then add *-s, -ed,* or *-ing* to the word in parentheses and complete the sentence using the word with the ending.

1. Yesterday, David _____ that he lost the key. (admit)

2. I have trouble _____ whether to take piano or karate. (decide)

3. The vice-principal _____ the supply closet each morning. (fill)

4. Are you _____ to include olives on the shopping list? (plan)

5. When Dad _____ to buy them, I am annoyed. (forget)

6. I hope Rudy _____ to walk the dog. (remember)

7. Last week's rain completely _____ the wicker chairs. (ruin)

8. If Amy is _____, we'll need to get going. (wait)

9. When you sneeze, she _____ her face with her arm. (cover)

10. Elvio _____ for the spaghetti last night. (ask)

**DIRECTIONS** Change the underlined verb in each sentence to the tense indicated. On the line, rewrite the sentence with the new tense so that it makes sense. You may need to add, delete, or change the spelling of some other words.

Change to present: Marlys kept calling the number listed in the directory.

11. _____

Change to in process: The phone rings, but no one answers.

12. _____

Change to past: Probably, the person who had that number was moving away.

13. _____

Change to in process: Lila tries to help Marlys get the information she needs.

14. _____

Change to present: The phone situation is preventing us from ordering the food.

15. _____

 Students apply grade-level phonics and word analysis skills.

Name _____

**DIRECTIONS** Write a sentence using each word.

neither     either

_____

_____

_____

_____

**Write in Response to Reading**

Reread "Harriet Tubman." How does reading the poem help you understand its theme? What ideas seem to be emphasized? Write your answer below, on a separate sheet of paper, or in a new document.

_____

_____

_____

_____

_____

_____

Students demonstrate contextual understanding of Benchmark Vocabulary. Students read text closely and use text evidence in their written answers.

**Evaluate Opinion**  Review *The Road to Freedom* and "Harriet Tubman," looking for perspectives from different people. Then evaluate how effectively the texts show different perspectives. Write an essay that presents your opinion about how the combined perspectives affect readers' understanding of Harriet Tubman. Write your essay on a separate sheet of paper, or start a new document.

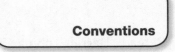

Conventions

## Independent Clauses

**DIRECTIONS**  On the line next to each sentence, identify whether it is a compound or complex sentence.

1.  My dog was happy to see me when I returned home. _____

2.  After we finished the game, the coach took us to a restaurant to celebrate. _____

3.  I'm looking for my mother, but I can't find her anywhere. _____

4.  Before we left for our trip, we checked the locks on all the doors and windows. _____

5.  My uncle is a chef and my aunt is a programmer. _____

Students write routinely for a range of tasks, purposes, and audiences. Students practice various conventions of standard English.

Name _____

**DIRECTIONS** Write a sentence using each word.

politics       rampant

_____

_____

_____

_____

**Write in Response to Reading**

Reread the last paragraph on page 73 and the first three paragraphs on page 74, starting with "See? I knew you wouldn't believe me." How do Cornelius and Otis feel about women running for office? Use dialogue from the passage and earlier in the story to write an explanatory paragraph. Write your answer below, on a separate sheet of paper, or in a new document.

_____

_____

_____

_____

_____

_____

Students demonstrate contextual understanding of Benchmark Vocabulary. Students read text closely and use text evidence in their written answers.

**Unit 2 • Module A • Lesson 12 • 135**

## Compare and Contrast Characters

**DIRECTIONS** Using evidence from the text, answer the following questions about pages 68–71 from *Operation Clean Sweep*.

1. Why is the narrator confused when he hears the women talking about nominations?

   _____

   _____

   _____

2. How do the narrator and Flora react differently to the suggestion that Flora be nominated for mayor?

   _____

   _____

3. How are the narrator's and Flora's views about the streetlights similar?

   _____

   _____

4. How are the narrator's and Flora's views about Elmer Diffenbottom's tombstone different?

   _____

   _____

   _____

Students analyze and respond to literary and informational text.

Name _____

**Plan a Speech** Plan and prewrite a speech about an injustice or inequality in your community or the world. On a separate sheet of paper or in a new document, complete a graphic organizer or write an outline to plan your speech. Be sure to include the topic and your opinion, your purpose and audience, and three reasons (in a logical order) that support your opinion.

**Conventions**

## Dependent Clauses

**DIRECTIONS** Underline the dependent clause in each complex sentence.

1. When women fought for suffrage, they faced many challenges.

2. Flora was pleased after her friends chose her to run for mayor.

3. If you see a place to park, let me know.

4. I injured my knee while we were playing soccer.

5. I love to eat *bulgogi,* which is a Korean beef dish.

Students write routinely for a range of tasks, purposes, and audiences. Students practice various conventions of standard English.

**DIRECTIONS** Write a sentence using each word.

tallied    underestimate

_____

_____

_____

_____

**Write in Response to Reading**

Reread the last paragraph on page 77. Do you think Dad should support the election of women or treat it as a joke and fight to get his job back? Use key details the author reveals about the character through his words, thoughts, and actions to write a paragraph explaining your opinion. Write your answer below, on a separate sheet of paper, or in a new document.

_____

_____

_____

_____

_____

Students demonstrate contextual understanding of Benchmark Vocabulary. Students read text closely and use text evidence in their written answers.

## On Loyalty to Country

Yesterday I walked the historic Freedom Trail in Boston. The Trail starts at the oldest park in the country, Boston Common, where British soldiers camped before the Revolutionary War. It ends at Bunker Hill, the site of the first major battle. The American Patriots worked hard for independence from England. Seeing Benjamin Franklin's statue, Paul Revere's house, and Faneuil Hall made me proud to be an American. Franklin was a political leader and signer of the Declaration of Independence. Revere made a legendary midnight ride to warn that the British were coming by sea. At Faneuil Hall, Samuel Adams gave speeches to inspire the colonists.

However, the Freedom Trail honors only those who worked for independence. My ancestors came from Great Britain in 1774. While they appreciated the opportunities they had in the colonies, they were also extremely proud of their home country. They remained loyal to England during the American Revolution. The rebels criticized them for being traitors, but the Loyalists believed they were right for being loyal to their ruler, King George III. Even William Franklin, Ben Franklin's son, supported England. He was a respected governor of New Jersey. Disagreement over patriotic loyalties resulted in a lifetime rift between the two men.

Loyalists believed a government that worked should not be replaced. Moreover, they felt the taxes they paid the British government were not extreme. They felt that those who protested were upset because they had not paid the taxes before. Some who wanted freedom from Great Britain believed the colonies did not have enough say in the decisions of Parliament. Yet, Loyalists argued, each colony had a governor who could send a representative to Great Britain to speak before Parliament.

Some questioned the rebels' tactics. For one, Adams wrote letters to newspapers signed with different names. He wanted to make it seem that everyone in the colonies desired independence. In fact, many colonists had not made up their minds about independence at the time the war broke out.

For these reasons, I propose that a statue be commissioned to represent a hero who fought on the side of Great Britain. One consideration could be Patrick Ferguson, who was an officer in the British Army. At the Battle of Brandywine in 1777, he acted with honor. He had an opportunity to shoot a rebel officer and did not. He later wrote that the thought of shooting someone in the back "disgusted" him. Some stories suggest that the rebel officer may have been George Washington!

Students read text closely to determine what the text says.

**Gather Evidence**  On page 139, underline three Loyalist arguments against independence, and circle one Patriot argument for independence.


**Gather Evidence: Extend Your Ideas**  Review the arguments you underlined and circled. Why do you think the author chose to write more Loyalist arguments and fewer Patriot arguments?

_____

_____

_____


**Ask Questions**  Write three questions a review board might ask about the proposal for the new statue.

_____

_____

_____


**Ask Questions: Extend Your Ideas**  Choose one of the three questions above about the statue. Bracket any details in the text that could answer your question, and write your response below. If you can't find any details in the text, create and answer a new question using specific ideas from the text.

_____

_____

_____


**Make Your Case**  Highlight details on page 139 that show a challenge Loyalists faced during the American Revolution. Next, using the highlighted detail, write a vivid sentence of your own to describe the challenge the Loyalists faced.

_____

_____

_____

 Students read text closely to determine what the text says.

**Draft a Speech**  Use the graphic organizer or outline you completed in Lesson 12 to draft your opinion speech. On a separate sheet of paper or in a new document, draft a speech that is engaging, interesting, and persuasive. Use devices such as repetition and figurative language to engage the audience and make important points. Include strong reasons and powerful evidence, but do not overload the speech with too many details. Keep your purpose and audience in mind as you draft your speech.

**Conventions**

## Connecting Independent Clauses

**DIRECTIONS**  Connect the two sentences in each item using *and, but,* or *or.*

1. Flora spoke. The women clapped and cheered.

   _____

2. We can make dinner. We can order pizza.

   _____

3. I want the large tablet. I cannot afford it.

   _____

4. He may go to the museum. He may go the aquarium.

   _____

5. Joanna went to the bank. It was not open yet.

   _____

Students write routinely for a range of tasks, purposes, and audiences. Students practice various conventions of standard English.

Name _____

**DIRECTIONS** Write a sentence using the word.

underestimate

_____

_____

_____

**Write in Response to Reading**

Write two or three explanatory paragraphs comparing and contrasting how government affects the lives of people in each story. Use details from both texts to explain. Write your answer on a separate sheet of paper or in a new document.

_____

_____

_____

_____

_____

Students demonstrate contextual understanding of Benchmark Vocabulary. Students read text closely and use text evidence in their written answers.

Name _____

## Compare and Contrast Stories

**DIRECTIONS** Using evidence from the texts, answer the following questions about *The Road to Freedom* and *Operation Clean Sweep*.

1. Consider the mothers in *The Road to Freedom* and *Operation Clean Sweep*. How are they similar, and how are they different?

    _____

    _____

2. How do the government and laws affect families in *The Road to Freedom* and *Operation Clean Sweep*?

    _____

    _____

    _____

    _____

    _____

    _____

3. How are the topics and perspectives presented in *The Road to Freedom* and *Operation Clean Sweep* similar?

    _____

    _____

4. Which story did you enjoy more? Give specific reasons for your answer, and support them with evidence from the text.

    _____

    _____

    _____

Students analyze and respond to literary and informational text.

Name _____

**Revise and Rewrite a Speech** On a separate sheet of paper or in a new document, make revisions to the draft of your opinion speech from Lesson 13. Use parallel structure and repetition to emphasize and clarify important reasons and ideas. Add transitions as necessary to show relationships between concepts or events. Replace vague or general language with precise words, and improve ineffective or unclear sentence structure. With a partner, peer review each other's drafts, making sure the organization makes sense and the language is strong. Finally, revise and rewrite your opinion speech based on your peer's feedback.

**Conventions**

## Subordinating Conjunctions

**DIRECTIONS** Using subordinating conjunctions from the box below, add a dependent clause to each sentence.

| after | although | because | before | if |
|-------|----------|---------|--------|-----|
| since | though | unless | when | while |

1. Escaped slaves' freedom remained in danger _____

   _____.

2. Abolitionists broke laws _____.

3. Harriet Tubman was so successful _____.

4. _____, they began to run for office.

5. _____, some men still did not see women as their equals.

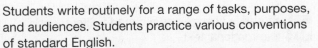

Students write routinely for a range of tasks, purposes, and audiences. Students practice various conventions of standard English.

**DIRECTIONS** Write a sentence using each word.

heritage     ironic

_____

_____

_____

_____

**Write in Response to Reading**

Do you agree that Cesar Chavez should have quit school to work in the fields with his family? Support your opinion with evidence from the text. Write your answer below, on a separate sheet of paper, or in a new document.

_____

_____

_____

_____

_____

_____

Students demonstrate contextual understanding of Benchmark Vocabulary.
Students read text closely and use text evidence in their written answers.

**Edit and Proofread a Speech** Exchange speeches with a new partner, and check for correct grammar, punctuation, capitalization, and spelling. Use the checklist below to guide you as you edit and proofread your partner's speech.

1. Check for correct use of correlative and subordinating conjunctions.

2. Check for effective use of interjections, if it makes sense to include them.

3. Check to correct sentence fragments.

4. Check that quotations are accurate and correctly punctuated.

5. Check for correct spelling, particularly of proper nouns and domain-specific words.

**Conventions**

## More Subordinating Conjunctions

**DIRECTIONS** Write a sentence using each of the following subordinating conjunctions.

1. after _____

_____

2. although _____

_____

3. before _____

_____

4. while _____

_____

5. whenever _____

_____

 Students write routinely for a range of tasks, purposes, and audiences. Students practice various conventions of standard English.

Name _____

## Shades of Meaning

**DIRECTIONS** For each set of three words, write three sentences that clearly illustrate the shades of meaning among the words. Use a dictionary to determine or clarify the meanings of the words.

**polite, outgoing, hospitable**

1. _____

2. _____

3. _____

**shade, gloom, darkness**

4. _____

5. _____

6. _____

**nibble, eat, devour**

7. _____

8. _____

9. _____

**belated, overdue, slow**

10. _____

11. _____

12. _____

**recall, relive, cherish**

13. _____

14. _____

15. _____

 Students apply grade-level phonics and word analysis skills.

Name _____

**DIRECTIONS** Write a sentence using the word.

convince

_____

_____

_____

_____

**Write in Response to Reading**

Reread the paragraphs on pages 96–98 under the subheadings "A Real Hero" and "Living On." How has Chavez been honored for his work? Use evidence from the text in your response. Write your answer below, on a separate sheet of paper, or in a new document.

_____

_____

_____

_____

_____

Students demonstrate contextual understanding of Benchmark Vocabulary. Students read text closely and use text evidence in their written answers.

**Present a Speech** Practice your speech in front of a partner or a small group of peers to improve your presentation. On a clean copy of your speech, mark the text to show where you will adjust your pace and tone to emphasize reasons, evidence, and interesting points. Also mark your speech to show when relevant visuals or multimedia will be displayed.

**Conventions**

## Correcting Sentence Fragments

**DIRECTIONS** On the line next to each item below, write *sentence* if it is complete and *fragment* if it is not. If the item is a fragment, rewrite the fragment as a complete sentence.

1. If Chavez had given up when organizing became frustrating. _____

   _____

   _____

   _____

2. Chavez was born into a loving family. _____

   _____

   _____

3. After the Great Depression closed many businesses. _____

   _____

   _____

Students write routinely for a range of tasks, purposes, and audiences. Students practice various conventions of standard English.

Name _____

**DIRECTIONS** Write a sentence using each word.

auction    quarters

_____

_____

_____

_____

**Write in Response to Reading**

In your opinion, which text's visuals best helped you understand how people respond to injustice? Use details from each text to support your opinion. Write your answer below, on a separate sheet of paper, or in a new document.

_____

_____

_____

_____

_____

Students demonstrate contextual understanding of Benchmark Vocabulary. Students read text closely and use text evidence in their written answers.

Name _____

## Compare and Contrast Visuals

**DIRECTIONS**  Using evidence from the texts, answer the following questions about *The Road to Freedom, Operation Clean Sweep,* and *Cesar Chavez: Champion of Workers.*

1.  Compare the homes in the visuals on page 45 of *The Road to Freedom* and page 83 of *Cesar Chavez: Champion of Workers.* How are they similar? How are the people who live in these homes similar?

    _____

    _____

2.  What is similar about the photograph on page 94 of *Cesar Chavez: Champion of Workers* and the illustration on page 76 of *Operation Clean Sweep?*

    _____

    _____

3.  Compare the visuals on pages 70–71 of *Operation Clean Sweep* to page 89 of *Cesar Chavez: Champion of Workers.* How are they similar? What do these similarities say about Flora and Cesar?

    _____

    _____

    _____

 Students analyze and respond to literary and informational text.

Name _____

**Research Leaders in History** Research a courageous leader who responded to injustice. On separate sheets of paper or in a new document, take notes on multiple sources. If relevant to your topic, use one text from this module. Include two or three additional print and digital sources. Use the leader's diary, public speeches, or autobiography as one source. Take notes on facts, record direct quotes, paraphrase and summarize each source's ideas, and credit each source by title and author in your notes.

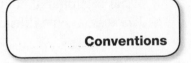

**Conventions**

## Correcting Run-on Sentences

**DIRECTIONS** Correct the following run-on sentences. Rewrite each sentence as two separate sentences or as a single sentence with a semicolon or a coordinating conjunction.

1. I really enjoyed reading the books in this unit, they taught me a lot about courage.

   _____

   _____

2. I like cats, they don't like me very much.

   _____

3. Carol went to the pharmacy, she needed to pick up some medicine.

   _____

   _____

 Students write routinely for a range of tasks, purposes, and audiences. Students practice various conventions of standard English.

Name _____

**DIRECTIONS** Write a sentence using each word.

tallied      heritage

_____

_____

_____

_____

**Write in Response to Reading**

Put into order the texts you have read in this module, from the text with the simplest text structure to the text with the most complex text structure. Explain the order you selected using evidence from the texts. Write your answer below, on a separate sheet of paper, or in a new document.

_____

_____

_____

_____

_____

Students demonstrate contextual understanding of Benchmark Vocabulary. Students read text closely and use text evidence in their written answers.

**Analyze Sources and Develop an Opinion**  On separate sheets of paper or in a new document, write a two-page opinion essay in which you use your research to develop an opinion about your chosen leader's most important contribution. First, decide on an opinion. Next, analyze your notes from the previous lesson, and identify supporting evidence. Then, draft your opinion essay. Make sure that your essay's organization is clear and that it includes reasons, supporting evidence, and a conclusion.

**Conventions**

## Spell Correctly

**DIRECTIONS**  Carefully read each word below, and write its correct spelling on the line.

1. releif _____

2. favrite _____

3. beleive _____

4. diffrent _____

5. arguement _____

 Students write routinely for a range of tasks, purposes, and audiences. Students practice various conventions of standard English.

## Greek and Latin Roots

### Word Bank

| | | | |
|---|---|---|---|
| erupt | subscription | interrupt | cycle |
| manuscript | eject | abrupt | cyclotron |
| injection | prescribe | project | respectfully |

**DIRECTIONS** Write the word from the Word Bank that has the same meaning.

1. purchase of a series of things
2. to burst out, as from a volcano
3. to write a rule or an order for medicine
4. machine sending particles around a circle
5. to stick out
6. unexpectedly sudden or steep
7. something forced into another thing
8. to break in
9. a piece of writing
10. events that repeat over and over
11. to push out
12. with an attitude of regard or esteem

1. _____
2. _____
3. _____
4. _____
5. _____
6. _____
7. _____
8. _____
9. _____
10. _____
11. _____
12. _____

**DIRECTIONS** Complete each sentence. Use a dictionary if you need some help.

13. *Ten* in Greek is *deka*; ten years equals one _____.

14. *Two* in Latin is *duo*; two people sing together in a _____.

15. *Eight* in Greek is *octo*; an eight-legged sea animal is an _____.

16. *One* in Latin is *unus*; another word for oneness is _____.

17. *Five* in Greek is *pente*; a shape with five sides is a _____.

Students apply grade-level phonics and word analysis skills.

Name _____

**DIRECTIONS** Write a sentence using each word.

superheroes    ridicule    welfare    entitled

_____

_____

_____

_____

_____

**Write in Response to Reading**

What are some differences between fictional superheroes and real-life superheroes such as Richard Martin? Give examples from the text as well as your own examples. Write your answer below, on a separate sheet of paper, or in a new document.

_____

_____

_____

_____

_____

_____

Students demonstrate contextual understanding of Benchmark Vocabulary. Students read text closely and use text evidence in their written answers.

**Introduce a Topic**  On a separate sheet of paper or in a new document, write an introduction to an informative essay about a real-life superhero of your choice. In this essay, you will explain who this person was and what he or she did to change the world, in detail. For now, your introduction should include background information on this person and why he or she is important. Be sure to clearly state a main idea and make an observation that focuses that topic.

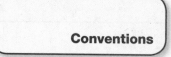

Conventions

## Subject-Verb Agreement

**DIRECTIONS**  Circle the subjects and underline the verbs in each sentence. If the subject and verb agree, write A on the line after the sentence. If they do not agree, write NA on the line, and rewrite the sentence so that it is correct.

**1.** They wants a better life.

_____

**2.** Callie, William, and Martha are hopeful.

_____

**3.** He go skiing every summer.

_____

**4.** Juanita reads the newspaper at breakfast every morning.

_____

**5.** You likes to play tennis, right?

_____

 Students write routinely for a range of tasks, purposes, and audiences. Students practice various conventions of standard English.

Name _____

**DIRECTIONS** Write a sentence using each word.

inherited     tenants     mistreated     cruelty

_____

_____

_____

_____

_____

_____

**Write in Response to Reading**

Look at the time line on page 4, and note where certain events in the text can be placed on the time line. Are events mentioned in the text in the same order that they would appear on the time line? Why do you think some events are not mentioned in the order in which they happened? Write your answer below, on a separate sheet of paper, or in a new document.

_____

_____

_____

_____

_____

Students demonstrate contextual understanding of Benchmark Vocabulary. Students read text closely and use text evidence in their written answers.

Name _____

## Text Structure

**DIRECTIONS** Using evidence from the text, answer the following questions about pages 7–10 from *Real-Life Superheroes*.

1. Look at the first paragraph on page 7. What important even happens in 1794? Why is it important?

   _____

   _____

2. Look at the second paragraph on page 8. How does its structure help you understand the time and effort it took Martin to change people's minds about treating animals kindly?

   _____

   _____

   _____

   _____

   _____

3. On page 9, the text states that in 1822, when Richard Martin was 68 years old, he finally got laws passed to protect animals. What does this use of chronological order help communicate about Richard Martin's character?

   _____

   _____

   _____

   _____

4. The introduction on pages 2–3 can be divided into three sections: the first describing superheroes, the second describing their actions, and the third describing the lasting results of these actions. Divide the text about Richard Martin on pages 4–10 into the same three groups.

   _____

   _____

Students analyze and respond to literary and informational text.

**Organize Ideas** Now use either chronological (sequence) or cause-effect structure to create an outline for your explanatory essay. If you choose chronological structure, decide which important events to include, and determine the time order of events. If you choose cause-effect structure, identify and list connected causes and effects. Causes and effects should be grouped logically. First, write your method of organization and your one-page outline on a separate sheet of paper or in a new document. Then, use your outline to begin drafting two or three paragraphs of your essay.

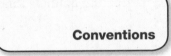

**Conventions**

### Subject-Verb Agreement: Phrases

**DIRECTIONS** Underline the word that correctly completes each sentence.

1. Her aunt with the children (was/were) never heard from again.

2. Runaways in a secret shelter (take/takes) big risks to become free.

3. The girl, unlike her brothers, (wear/wears) eyeglasses.

4. A horse with stripes (is/are) called a zebra.

5. The cards in this deck (have/has) been marked to help the magician perform her trick.

 Students write routinely for a range of tasks, purposes, and audiences. Students practice various conventions of standard English.

Name _____

**DIRECTIONS** Write a sentence using each word.

missionary    poverty    destitute    affected

_____

_____

_____

_____

_____

**Write in Response to Reading**

Read the section "The First of Many" on page 14. What does *raised* mean in this context? What are some other words or phrases that use *raise* in this way? Write your answer below, on a separate sheet of paper, or in a new document.

_____

_____

_____

_____

_____

Students demonstrate contextual understanding of Benchmark Vocabulary. Students read text closely and use text evidence in their written answers.

## Bound for Kansas!

Jefferson Wilson was born into slavery in the South. The North's victory in the Civil War had promised opportunities for a better life, but the realities had fallen far short of what he expected. For all intents and purposes, as sharecroppers, Wilson and other former slaves were not truly free. No wonder they were dissatisfied with life in their Tennessee town.

A white man owned the land that Jefferson Wilson, his wife, and his three sons worked. The rent was so high and the rates for crops so low that his family was constantly in debt. The same was true for all sharecroppers. Living conditions were harsh, and racial tensions made Wilson worry for the safety of his family.

One day as he walked through Nashville, Jefferson Wilson spotted an advertisement for homesteading in Kansas. An acquaintance of his, businessman Benjamin Singleton, had posted it. Wilson investigated further and soon realized that he could afford transportation for his family if he didn't buy seeds for another year of sharecropping. After long discussions with friends and family—many of whom chose to stay in Tennessee—the Wilsons decided to head west with Mr. Singleton and one other family to help establish the all-black community of Dunlap, Kansas. The journey was long and difficult, with yellow fever claiming the lives of several travelers. Hopes of finding new opportunities sustained the pioneers.

When the Wilsons arrived, they faced many physical and emotional challenges. Farming the Kansas land proved difficult, and they were lonely. But one thing made all the difference—Jefferson Wilson and his neighbors owned the land they worked and the houses they built. It was theirs. Though they experienced some discrimination in Kansas, they no longer lived in constant fear for their lives.

The community established its own school—The Dunlap Academy and Mission School—which Wilson was proud to say his sons attended. As time passed, more and more people came to Dunlap, creating a tight-knit community of hundreds of black families.

Despite the difficulties of constructing their sod house and clearing ground to plant, Jefferson Wilson and his wife never regretted their decision to begin a new life in Kansas. Eventually, their crops prospered, and life became easier. They had sacrificed a lot to start over, but they knew they had made the right choice for their family. Most importantly, they finally knew what freedom truly meant.

 Students read text closely to determine what the text says.

**Gather Evidence**  What made Jefferson Wilson want to move from Tennessee to Kansas? Underline three text details that explain Jefferson Wilson's actions.

**Gather Evidence: Extend Your Ideas**  Review the text details you underlined. What conclusion can you draw about the conditions in Tennessee and Kansas?

_____

_____

_____

**Ask Questions**  What information would help you understand what life was like in Kansas? Circle three details related to homesteading in Kansas that you would like to know more about.

**Ask Questions: Extend Your Ideas**  Choose one of the three topics you would like to know more about, and bracket two details in the text that are related to it.

**Make Your Case**  In what time period does this story take place? Highlight three clues in the text that relate to the time period.

**Make Your Case: Extend Your Ideas**  How does knowing the setting of the story help you better understand the events in it? Discuss your results with a partner.

_____

_____

_____

_____

Students read text closely to determine what the text says.

Name _____

**Use Quotations to Develop a Topic**  Select several quotations related to your chosen real-life superhero from the texts in the unit or outside texts. Be sure to choose quotations that use particularly powerful language. On separate sheets of paper or in a new document, incorporate each quotation into a body paragraph and explain why the quotation supports a main point of the essay. Use these paragraphs to add one to two pages to your explanatory essay from the previous lessons.

**Conventions**

## Subject-Verb Agreement: Indefinite Pronouns

**DIRECTIONS**  *Everybody, neither,* and *someone* are examples of singular indefinite pronouns. *Few, several,* and *other* are examples of plural indefinite pronouns. *All, none,* and *some* may be singular or plural. Underline the correct verb in each sentence.

1. Everybody (has/have) one bag for the journey.

2. Some of the people (wants/want) a meeting before leaving.

3. Excuse me, someone (is/are) calling my cell phone.

4. Most marsupials are found in Australia; few (lives/live) elsewhere.

 Students write routinely for a range of tasks, purposes, and audiences. Students practice various conventions of standard English.

Name _____

**DIRECTIONS** Write a sentence using each word.

tragedy    foster    charity

_____

_____

_____

_____

**Write in Response to Reading**

The introduction to the text offers a number of traits shared by real-life superheroes: they rely on inner strengths like determination and bravery, they face opposition and even danger for standing up for their beliefs, and they create lasting change in the world. Find three specific examples in the text of ways Thomas Barnardo demonstrated each of these traits. Be as specific as possible, giving names, dates, and locations when possible. Write your answer below, on a separate sheet of paper, or in a new document.

_____

_____

_____

_____

_____

Students demonstrate contextual understanding of Benchmark Vocabulary. Students read text closely and use text evidence in their written answers.

**Locate Key Information**

**DIRECTIONS** Using evidence from the text, answer the following questions about pages 15–17 from *Real-Life Superheroes*.

1. What important decision does Barnardo make in the section "A Terrible Tragedy"?

   _____

   _____

2. How does Barnardo expand his work in the section "A New Venture"?

   _____

   _____

3. Why is Barnardo's Copperfield Road Ragged School unique?

   _____

   _____

4. What does the section "Hard Work" communicate about the lasting effects of Barnardo's work?

   _____

   _____

5. What does the section "Continuing His Care" communicate about the impact of Barnardo's work?

   _____

   _____

   _____

   _____

   _____

Students analyze and respond to literary and informational text.

**Develop a Topic with Facts and Details** Conduct research to find additional information about the real-life superhero you have chosen to write about. Focus on the impact this person had on other people. Using a separate sheet of paper or a new document, incorporate these facts, details, and examples into your explanatory essay from the previous lessons. Check that each paragraph includes a general topic sentence, followed by relevant facts and detail.

**Conventions**

## Subject-Verb Agreement: Collective Nouns

**DIRECTIONS** Underline the correct verb in each sentence.

1. The team (is/are) going to the playoffs.

2. His group (has/have) three members.

3. The family (was/were) in separate cars.

4. In soccer, two teams (tries/try) to control a ball using their feet.

5. A committee of residents (makes/make) decisions regarding neighborhood rules and policies.

 Students write routinely for a range of tasks, purposes, and audiences. Students practice various conventions of standard English.

Name _____

**DIRECTIONS** Write a sentence using each word.

diplomat    persecution    deported

_____

_____

_____

_____

**Write in Response to Reading**

In many cases, first-person point of view is considered "stronger" at conveying emotions than third-person point of view. Why might the writer have preferred third person for this text, especially in the section about Raoul Wallenberg? Write your answer below, on a separate sheet of paper, or in a new document.

_____

_____

_____

_____

_____

Students demonstrate contextual understanding of Benchmark Vocabulary. Students read text closely and use text evidence in their written answers.

Name _____

**Develop a Topic with Domain-Specific Vocabulary** Continue developing your explanatory essay. Look at the body paragraphs you have already written, and replace vague or general language with domain-specific vocabulary wherever you can. On separate sheets of paper or in a new document, write one to two additional pages, using precise language and domain-specific vocabulary. Consider your audience's historical knowledge, and write definitions, examples, and explanations when necessary.

**Conventions**

### Subject-Verb Agreement: Special Nouns

**DIRECTIONS** Write a sentence with each noun below as the subject and correct subject-verb agreement.

1. physics _____

2. gymnastics _____

3. politics _____

4. mathematics _____

Students write routinely for a range of tasks, purposes, and audiences. Students practice various conventions of standard English.

**Suffixes *-tion, -ion***

**DIRECTIONS** For each word, write the base word and show how its spelling changed when the suffix was added. For example, for the word *abrasion*, you would write *abrade + sion*.

1. initiation _____

2. exhibition _____

3. formation _____

4. vacation _____

5. emission _____

6. revision _____

7. immersion _____

8. possession _____

9. introduction _____

10. conversation _____

11. tension _____

12. relaxation _____

13. graduation _____

14. explosion _____

15. division _____

16. expansion _____

17. reservation _____

18. persuasion _____

19. explanation _____

20. compression _____

 Students apply grade-level phonics word and word analysis skills.

Name _____

**DIRECTIONS** Write a sentence using each word.

authorities    convince    campaign    sacrifice

_____

_____

_____

_____

_____

_____

**Write in Response to Reading**

Raoul Wallenberg was born in Sweden, but page 24 shows a statue of him in London. Why do you think he has a statue there? Write your answer below, on a separate sheet of paper, or in a new document.

_____

_____

_____

_____

_____

_____

Students demonstrate contextual understanding of Benchmark Vocabulary. Students read text closely and use text evidence in their written answers.

**Develop a Topic with Visuals and Text Features** On a separate sheet of paper or in a new document, add formatting to your explanatory essay to clarify its organization, including section breaks and section headings. Then conduct research to add relevant visuals. Find primary sources such as posters, photographs, and advertisements, and include captions and labels for these sources.

**Conventions**

## Subject-Verb Agreement: Inverted Sentences

**DIRECTIONS** Underline the correct verb for each sentence.

1. There (is/are) many questions.

2. There (is/are) a risk involved for everyone.

3. (Was/Were) we to continue traveling on that road, we would end up in St. Louis.

4. How many cats (is/are) your sister taking care of?

5. How much sugar (does/do) you want in your coffee?

Students write routinely for a range of tasks, purposes, and audiences. Students practice various conventions of standard English.

Name _____

### Suffix -ous

**DIRECTIONS** Complete each sentence by adding the suffix *-ous* to the noun in parentheses. You will probably have to change the spelling of the base word. Check your spelling in a dictionary if you wish.

1. During the night, there was an _____ snowstorm. (enormity)

2. Toby thought the news about school was _____. (marvel)

3. He could do something _____, like making a snow fort. (ambition)

4. He could do something _____, like building a silly-looking snowman. (humor)

5. As he dressed, he considered _____ possibilities. (variety)

6. The high school was starting on time, which she found _____. (ridicule)

7. As the two stepped outside, Tabitha gave Toby a _____ shove. (vigor)

8. He fell into the snow, but it felt _____ to him. (glory)

9. Whatever he did with the extra time, he knew he was _____. (victory)

10. Toby gave his sister a _____ bow as she trudged off. (courtesy)

Students apply grade-level phonics and word analysis skills.

Name _____

**DIRECTIONS** Write a sentence using each word.

segregated     discrimination     privacy     protest

_____

_____

_____

_____

_____

_____

**Write in Response to Reading**

A snowball effect is when a small cause creates a big effect, similar to a snowball rolling down a hill and getting bigger as more snow sticks to it. Explain how Rosa Parks's story is an example of a snowball effect. Can you think of other examples? Write your answer below, on a separate sheet of paper, or in a new document.

_____

_____

_____

_____

_____

Students demonstrate contextual understanding of Benchmark Vocabulary. Students read text closely and use text evidence in their written answers.

**Use Transitions to Link Information** On a separate sheet of paper or in a new document, add two to three pages to the draft of your explanatory essay, using transitions to link ideas. Remember to use appropriate transitions to indicate structure, for example, cause-effect, problem-solution, chronological order, or compare-contrast.

Conventions

## Punctuating Items in a Series: Commas

**DIRECTIONS** Insert commas into the correct places in the following series.

1. Fugitives found work in various jobs, such as cook deckhand minister nurse and printer.

2. The dinner special comes with a side of chicken noodle soup Caesar salad macaroni and cheese or french fries.

3. On Sunshine Cruises, you can eat play and relax all day!

4. Terrance Claudia Stephanie and I played doubles tennis last weekend.

5. My brothers my sister and I watched a movie had dinner at our favorite restaurant and played card games.

 Students write routinely for a range of tasks, purposes, and audiences. Students practice various conventions of standard English.

Name _____

**DIRECTIONS** Write a sentence using each word.

exodus    momentous    adversity

_____

_____

_____

_____

**Write in Response to Reading**

Reread the first full paragraph on page 2. Use the information from your completed graphic organizer to write an explanatory paragraph about the process Lawrence used in painting the *Migration* series. Write your answer below, on a separate sheet of paper, or in a new document.

_____

_____

_____

_____

_____

_____

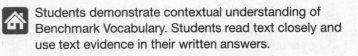

Students demonstrate contextual understanding of Benchmark Vocabulary. Students read text closely and use text evidence in their written answers.

Name _____

## Main Idea and Key Details

**DIRECTIONS** Using evidence from the text, answer the following questions about the introduction to *The Great Migration.*

1. Write a summary of the introduction, including only the main ideas. Include one quotation from the text.

   _____

   _____

   _____

   _____

   _____

   _____

2. Explain the importance of the detail "Harlem was crowded with newcomers" in your own words.

   _____

   _____

   _____

   _____

3. Based on the ideas in the introduction, make a prediction about the characters that will appear in this book.

   _____

   _____

4. Quote a phrase or sentence from the introduction that supports the main idea *The author has a personal relationship with the topic of the book.*

   _____

   _____

Students analyze and respond to literary and informational text.

**Develop a Conclusion** On a separate sheet of paper or in a new document, complete your draft and write a conclusion. Make sure your conclusion summarizes the main ideas and explains why the topic is important, answers or poses a question, or quotes a person closely connected with the topic.

Conventions

## Punctuating Items in a Series: Semicolons

**DIRECTIONS** Rewrite the following sentences, adding punctuation where needed.

1. The Great Migration brought people to Atlantic City New Jersey Pittsburgh Pennsylvania and Detroit Michigan.

   _____

   _____

   _____

2. Sarah will bring the grill and charcoal Jeff will bring the hot dogs buns and chips and Greta and will bring the ketchup mustard and soda.

   _____

   _____

   _____

3. We will visit Barcelona Spain Turin Italy and Berlin Germany.

   _____

   _____

 Students write routinely for a range of tasks, purposes, and audiences. Students practice various conventions of standard English.

Name _____

**DIRECTIONS** Write a sentence using each word.

ravaged     barren

_____

_____

_____

_____

**Write in Response to Reading**

Write an opinion paragraph about whether descriptive details effectively convey the text's power and emotion to the reader. Write your answer below, on a separate sheet of paper, or in a new document.

_____

_____

_____

_____

_____

_____

Students demonstrate contextual understanding of
Benchmark Vocabulary. Students read text closely
and use text evidence in their written answers.

**Compare and Contrast Visuals** On a separate sheet of paper or in a new document, write a one- to two-page essay to compare and contrast visuals in *Real-Life Superheroes* and *The Great Migration*. First, consider the types of visuals and the purposes they serve in each text. Then compare and contrast the visuals using a Venn diagram. Organize your essay in point-by-point or block structure, and include transitions to indicate similarities and differences.

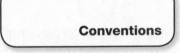

**Conventions**

## Commas with Introductory Elements

**DIRECTIONS** Add commas where needed in the sentences below.

1. In some places entire communities left their homes to move north.

2. As he did every morning Colin made a simple breakfast and ate it while reading the news.

3. Unlike my siblings I did not require braces while growing up.

4. While many people prefer the excitement of the city David has always enjoyed the countryside more.

5. Despite its name a glass snake is actually a type of legless lizard.

Students write routinely for a range of tasks, purposes, and audiences. Students practice various conventions of standard English.

**DIRECTIONS** Write a sentence using each word.

agents     confined

_____

_____

_____

_____

**Write in Response to Reading**

How do *The Great Migration* and "Migration" (on the last page of the book) portray the movement of African Americans from the South to the North? Use evidence from both texts to support your answer. Write your answer below, on a separate sheet of paper, or in a new document.

_____

_____

_____

_____

_____

Students demonstrate contextual understanding of Benchmark Vocabulary. Students read text closely and use text evidence in their written answers.

## Multiple Accounts of an Event

**DIRECTIONS**  Using evidence from the text, answer the following questions about pages 24–47 from *The Great Migration* and the poem "Migration."

1.  What kinds of jobs did African Americans take when they migrated north?

    _____

    _____

2.  Who were the people who opposed the Great Migration, and why were they against it?

    _____

    _____

3.  What are some of the benefits of moving to the North?

    _____

    _____

4.  Look at the poem "Migration." What are some of the things people brought with them?

    _____

    _____

5.  What information and ideas does "Migration" add to *The Great Migration*?

    _____

    _____

Students analyze and respond to literary and informational text.

Name _____

**Research a Topic**  Go to the library to research an inspirational person from the unit. Find at least three sources, including both primary and secondary sources, about this person. Write one to two pages of notes on your sources, and include the following information about each source: author, publisher, date of publication (for print sources), and Web site and date of access (for Web sources). Use a separate sheet of paper or start a new document.

**Conventions**

## Commas with *Yes* and *No*

**DIRECTIONS**  Answer the following questions while correctly demonstrating the use of a comma to set off the words *yes* and *no*.

1.  Do you have any brothers or sisters?

    _____

2.  Do you have any pets?

    _____

3.  Have you ever eaten sushi?

    _____

4.  Can you wiggle your ears?

    _____

5.  Are you left-handed?

    _____

Students write routinely for a range of tasks, purposes, and audiences. Students practice various conventions of standard English.

**Compound Words**

**DIRECTIONS** Write the two words that make up each compound word.

1. bellybutton _____ _____

2. ingrown _____ _____

3. homestead _____ _____

4. standpoint _____ _____

5. waterproof _____ _____

**DIRECTIONS** Write a definition for each compound word based on the meanings of the two words that make up each compound word. Use a dictionary if needed.

6. heavyweight _____

7. freestyle _____

8. cornhusk _____

9. timepiece _____

10. uppermost _____

**DIRECTIONS** Combine a word from the left and a word from the right into a compound word that matches each definition.

| | |
|------|-------|
| flex | over |
| pin | down |
| stop | wheel |
| clamp | time |

11. an action that imposes restrictions, rules, or control _____

12. allowing employees to set their own work hours _____

13. the place one rests in the middle of a trip _____

14. a toy with spinning arms attached to a stick _____

Copyright © Pearson Education, Inc., or its affiliates. All Rights Reserved.

Students apply grade-level phonics and word analysis skills.

Name _____

**DIRECTIONS** Write a sentence using each word.

mistreated    affected    exodus

_____

_____

_____

_____

**Write in Response to Reading**

Which structure do you think is more appealing to the reader—the structure of *Real-Life Superheroes* or that of *The Great Migration*? Use details from each text to support your opinion. Write your answer below, on a separate sheet of paper, or in a new document.

_____

_____

_____

_____

_____

Students demonstrate contextual understanding of Benchmark Vocabulary. Students read text closely and use text evidence in their written answers.

Name _____

**Evaluate Sources**  On a separate sheet of paper or in a new document, write a one-to two-page evaluation of your sources. First, write a brief analysis of each source's reliability based on the author's background and purpose, the publication date and, for Web sources, the site's URL. Then synthesize the sources, emphasizing how different sources shed light on different aspects of the topic. Consider whether various facts are verified by more than one source. Finally, conclude by writing a Works Cited list showing which sources you plan to use in the presentation you will write in Lessons 12 and 13.

**Conventions**

## Commas with Tag Questions

**DIRECTIONS**  Read the sentences and add commas where needed.

1. They asked, "There's more to the story isn't there?"

2. We have enough bread cheese and meat for sandwiches don't we?

3. You didn't delete the original files yet did you?

4. Before you left the house you locked the door didn't you?

5. There's no more spaghetti left is there?

 Students write routinely for a range of tasks, purposes, and audiences. Students practice various conventions of standard English.

**DIRECTIONS** Write a sentence using the word.

guardian

_____

_____

_____

_____

**Write in Response to Reading**

Reread the two paragraphs on pages 101–102. Use the information from your completed graphic organizer to write an informative paragraph summarizing the main ideas and supporting key details in these two paragraphs. Make sure to present the information in your own words. Write your answer below, on a separate sheet of paper, or in a new document.

_____

_____

_____

_____

_____

Students demonstrate contextual understanding of Benchmark Vocabulary. Students read text closely and use text evidence in their written answers.

Name _____

## Main Idea and Details

**DIRECTIONS**  Using evidence from the text, answer the following questions from pages 100–101 from *Angel Island.*

1. Look at page 100. What feature on the page introduces the topic?

   _____

2. Look at page 100. What idea in the text does the map support?

   _____

   _____

3. Look at page 100. How does the caption on the map relate to the information in the text?

   _____

   _____

   _____

4. Is the name of the explorer who named the island a key detail? Why or why not?

   _____

   _____

   _____

   _____

5. What inference can you make based on the photo and caption on page 101? Cite evidence from the text to support your answer.

   _____

   _____

   _____

Students analyze and respond to literary and informational text.

**Plan an Informative Presentation**  On a separate sheet of paper or in a new document, plan an informative presentation about the person you researched in Lesson 10. First, determine your presentation's purpose and audience. Then, take notes on how to organize the main sections of your presentation. In your notes, identify text features and multimedia components to include.

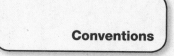

**Conventions**

## Commas to Indicate Direct Address

**DIRECTIONS**  Write five sentences using direct address, placing commas where needed.

1. _____

2. _____

3. _____

4. _____

5. _____

 Students write routinely for a range of tasks, purposes, and audiences. Students practice various conventions of standard English.

Name _____

**DIRECTIONS** Write a sentence using the word.

discrimination

_____

_____

_____

_____

**Write in Response to Reading**

Reread pages 103–104 and review the information in your graphic organizer. Which reasons and evidence about the topic of Chinese immigrants coming to the United States do you think would be most interesting to readers? Use text details to support your opinion. Write your answer below, on a separate sheet of paper, or in a new document.

_____

_____

_____

_____

_____

_____

Students demonstrate contextual understanding of Benchmark Vocabulary. Students read text closely and use text evidence in their written answers.

## A Voice for Women

In 1815, when Elizabeth Cady Stanton was born in Johnstown, New York, males had much more influence and many more options for employment than females in the United States. American women could not become government leaders, preachers, or professors. Girls with an interest in public speaking or politics were steered in other directions. The law even barred women from voting. Like other girls of her time, Elizabeth was expected to become a wife and mother when she grew up—and not much else.

It's not surprising that Elizabeth Cady Stanton eventually became a wife and mother. Though she loved her family, Stanton was passionate about politics as well. One of her causes was the effort to abolish slavery in the United States. Before her marriage in 1840, moreover, she had made supporting this movement a priority. Following her marriage, she and her husband attended an antislavery conference in England.

Stanton's main concern, though, was fair treatment for women. In the mid-1800s, the laws recognized few rights of American women. Besides being barred from voting, women could not serve on juries and were denied an equal education. Women could not divorce their husbands. In 1848, Stanton helped organize the Women's Rights Convention in Seneca Falls, New York. She wrote a declaration of women's rights, which was passed by the convention's delegates. This document demanded that the same rights be recognized for women as for men.

By the 1860s, Stanton was speaking and writing frequently about women's rights. Many Americans—men and women alike—disagreed with her positions. Some mocked her, while others simply ignored her. Standing strong in her beliefs, Stanton continued to travel extensively, making speeches and trying to change people's minds.

Stanton had disagreements with people on her side too. After the Civil War, which ended slavery in 1865, most women's rights advocates supported granting voting rights to African Americans. Yet, when politicians decided to allow black men to vote— while continuing to keep women of all races from voting—Stanton became furious, adamantly refusing to support voting rights for African American men if women could not vote. Many other women's rights activists, however, disagreed with her. The result was a split; from 1869 to 1890, the women's rights movement formed two competing organizations.

Fighting for women's rights into her old age, Stanton inspired thousands of Americans. Though she died in 1902, eighteen years later the United States approved the Nineteenth Amendment, which at last recognized women's right to vote.

Students read text closely to determine what the text says.

**Gather Evidence** Underline three phrases that describe the legal status of American women in the 1800s.

**Gather Evidence: Extend Your Ideas** Look at the underlined text. Circle three actions that Elizabeth Cady Stanton took to change the status of women.

**Ask Questions** Highlight one topic related to women's rights that you would like to know more about.

**Ask Questions: Extend Your Ideas** Look at the topic you chose. Write two questions that you could answer by doing research.

_____

_____

**Make Your Case** What conclusion can you draw about laws in the United States in the 1800s? Bracket an example from the text to support your answer.

_____

_____

**Make Your Case: Extend Your Ideas** Name one short-term effect and one long-term effect of Elizabeth Cady Stanton's actions, and give dates for each. Discuss your results with a partner.

_____

_____

_____

Students read text closely to determine what the text says.

**Draft an Informative Presentation**  On a separate sheet of paper or in a new document, draft three to five sections/slides of your informative presentation. First, refer to your Lesson 12 plans to review how the main sections are organized. Then, determine key points and facts you want to include in each section. Finally, write sentences or bullet points that present information from your research in an engaging way.

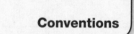

**Conventions**

### Underline Titles of Works

**DIRECTIONS**  Underline the titles of works in the following sentences.

1. Did you read Night of the Spadefoot Toads and Real-Life Superheroes?

2. My grandfather loved reading Grimms' Fairy Tales.

3. The Epic of Gilgamesh is one of the oldest works of literature.

4. Inferno, Purgatorio, and Paradiso compose The Divine Comedy, which was written by Dante Alighieri.

5. Treasure Island, Kidnapped, and Strange Case of Dr. Jekyll and Mr. Hyde are three of Robert Louis Stevenson's most famous novels.

Students write routinely for a range of tasks, purposes, and audiences. Students practice various conventions of standard English.

Name _____

**DIRECTIONS** Write a sentence using each word.

quotas    persecution

_____

_____

_____

_____

**Write in Response to Reading**

How does the imagery used in the third paragraph on page 106 help the reader understand the plight of the Chinese immigrants? Write an explanatory paragraph on this topic. Write your answer below, on a separate sheet of paper, or in a new document.

_____

_____

_____

_____

_____

Students demonstrate contextual understanding of Benchmark Vocabulary. Students read text closely and use text evidence in their written answers.

Name _____

## Craft and Structure

**DIRECTIONS**  Using evidence from the text, answer the following questions about pages 106–107 from *Angel Island*.

1.  How does the author's use of chronological order affect the reader?

    _____

    _____

2.  How would the effect differ if the author used cause-effect structure?

    _____

    _____

    _____

3.  What does the author's word choice in the last full paragraph on page 106 help you understand about the experience of Chinese immigrants in the late 1800s?

    _____

    _____

    _____

4.  Look at the second full paragraph on page 107. Why does the author include a quotation?

    _____

    _____

Students analyze and respond to literary and informational text.

Name _____

**Revise or Rewrite an Informative Presentation** Exchange drafts with a partner. On a separate sheet of paper or in a new document, take notes and make suggestions for your partner by answering the following questions about your partner's draft:

1. What organizational structure is used? Is the organization effective?

2. Are there vague or general words that could be replaced with more precise words?

3. Could a quote from a source or a visual add authenticity and make the informative presentation come alive?

4. What visuals would help clarify information or support points?

After getting your partner's feedback, revise your presentation.

**Conventions**

## Italics for Titles of Works

**DIRECTIONS** Write a short paragraph explaining what type of titles should be put in italics. Provide examples of titles that should and should not be italicized.

_____

_____

_____

_____

_____

Students write routinely for a range of tasks, purposes, and audiences. Students practice various conventions of standard English.

Name _____

**DIRECTIONS** Write a sentence using each word.

authorities ensure

_____

_____

_____

**Write in Response to Reading**

Review what you learned about the relationships and interactions between people and events on pages 108–109 and the first paragraph on page 110. Was the 1906 San Francisco earthquake and fire a complete disaster or lucky for some people? Write a paragraph responding to this question, using details from the text to support your opinion. Write your answer below, on a separate sheet of paper, or in a new document.

_____

_____

_____

_____

_____

Students demonstrate contextual understanding of Benchmark Vocabulary. Students read text closely and use text evidence in their written answers.

**Edit and Proofread an Informative Presentation**  Exchange drafts of your informative presentation with a partner. Using the checklist below, edit and proofread your partner's presentation.

- ❑ Correct grammar, including subject-verb agreement
- ❑ Correct punctuation
- ❑ Correct capitalization
- ❑ Correct spelling

Use a dictionary or reference source to verify spellings, in particular the spellings of proper nouns and historical terms. Use a separate sheet of paper or start a new document.

**Conventions**

## Quotation Marks for Titles of Works

**DIRECTIONS**  Rewrite the sentences using the correct punctuation.

1. Walter Dean Myers wrote the poem Migration.

   _____

2. My aunt's song You Are a Star is on the radio.

   _____

3. Open your books to the section Proving Citizenship.

   _____

4. The episode Cheetahs won several awards.

   _____

5. The Tortoise and the Hare is my favorite fable.

   _____

 Students write routinely for a range of tasks, purposes, and audiences. Students practice various conventions of standard English.

**Prefixes *pre-*, *re-***

### Word Bank

| | | | | |
|---|---|---|---|---|
| construction | placed | views | freeze | occupied |
| measured | arrange | pack | decorate | ordered |
| match | sale | phrase | rehearsed | set |

**DIRECTIONS** Add *pre-* or *re-* to a word from the Word Bank to complete each sentence.

1. She _____ the book before it was officially published.

2. He had to _____ the flowers after they were delivered.

3. The _____ did not accurately represent the movie.

4. I prefer to _____ the oven temperature so that it warms up.

5. After the tornado, the area underwent a lot of _____.

6. You should donate your old hats to the _____ shop.

7. Let me _____ that muddled sentence.

8. Dmitri _____ the nails he had borrowed from the store.

9. Ann's speech at our first practice session sounded _____.

10. The piecrust ingredients were all _____.

**DIRECTIONS** Add *pre-* or *re-* to a word from the Word Bank to match each definition.

11. put items into a suitcase before the day of departure _____

12. put a thawed piece of food into the freezer again _____

13. a new contest with the same two competitors _____

14. caught up in one's own thoughts _____

15. put up new artwork and curtains _____

Students apply grade-level phonics and word analysis skills.

Name _____

**DIRECTIONS** Write a sentence using each word.

accompanied     withheld     sacrifices

_____

_____

_____

**Write in Response to Reading**

What effect does the writer's use of figurative language have on the overall meaning of the text? Write an explanatory paragraph below, on a separate sheet of paper, or in a new document.

_____

_____

_____

_____

_____

Students demonstrate contextual understanding of Benchmark Vocabulary. Students read text closely and use text evidence in their written answers.

**Publish and Present an Informative Presentation** Prepare your informational presentation using your work from Lessons 12–15. Find and cut out photos, graphs, maps, charts, and other visuals to enhance your presentation. If available, use publishing software to add visuals and create layouts digitally. If not, use separate sheets of paper to create layouts, including text and images, by hand. Include facts and relevant descriptive details. Focus on main ideas and interesting points as you give your presentation. Speak clearly at an understandable pace.

**Conventions**

## Titles of Works

**DIRECTIONS** Write *underlining, italics,* or *quotation marks* on the blank line next to each item to indicate how to correctly punctuate the title.

1. Handwritten title of a poem that is included in an anthology: _____

2. Handwritten title of a movie: _____

3. Typed title of an article from a magazine: _____

4. Typed title of a magazine or newspaper: _____

5. Typed title of a book of poetry: _____

Students write routinely for a range of tasks, purposes, and audiences. Students practice various conventions of standard English.

Name _____

**DIRECTIONS** Write a sentence using each word.

discrimination     persecution     sacrifices

_____

_____

_____

_____

_____

_____

**Write in Response to Reading**

Which text uses tone and voice more effectively to help readers understand individuals' emotional responses to events? Use details from each text to support your opinion. Write your answer below, on a separate sheet of paper, or in a new document.

_____

_____

_____

_____

_____

Students demonstrate contextual understanding of Benchmark Vocabulary. Students read text closely and use text evidence in their written answers.

Name _____

## Text Structure and Tone

**DIRECTIONS** Using evidence from the texts, answer the following questions about *Real-Life Superheroes* and *Angel Island.*

1. What is the connection between text structure and author's purpose in each text?

   _____

   _____

   _____

2. What is the connection between tone and author's purpose in each text?

   _____

   _____

   _____

3. How does the text structure in each text help develop its tone?

   _____

   _____

   _____

   _____

Students analyze and respond to literary and informational text.

Name _____

**Analyze Reasons and Evidence** On a separate sheet of paper or in a new document, take notes on how the author uses reasons and evidence to support points in the introduction for *The Great Migration*. Then write two pages that analyze how the author uses reasons and evidence to support his points. Be sure to identify which reasons and evidence support which points, and include an evaluation of the effectiveness of the author's techniques.

**Conventions**

## Spelling Correctly

**DIRECTIONS** Look at the words below. If the word is spelled correctly, write *correct* on the blank line. If the word is not spelled correctly, rewrite it correctly on the blank line.

1. achievement _____

2. changable _____

3. independant _____

4. judgement _____

5. experience _____

Students write routinely for a range of tasks, purposes, and audiences. Students practice various conventions of standard English.

Name _____

**DIRECTIONS** Write a sentence using each word.

momentous     adversity     authorities

_____

_____

_____

_____

**Write in Response to Reading**

Choose a different topic that appears in all three texts, such as *the meaning of freedom.* Then use information from the texts to write an informative paragraph comparing and contrasting the topic across the three texts. Include facts and key details from each text to integrate information about the topic. Write your answer below, on a separate sheet of paper, or in a new document.

_____

_____

_____

_____

_____

_____

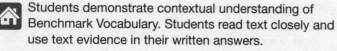
Students demonstrate contextual understanding of Benchmark Vocabulary. Students read text closely and use text evidence in their written answers.

Name _____

**Compare and Contrast Texts** Draft an essay comparing and contrasting how *The Great Migration* and *Angel Island* present the migration experience. Include a clear introduction, logically organized points to compare and contrast how the texts address the topic, evidence from each text to support stated points, transitions to show comparisons (e.g., *like, both*) and contrasts (e.g., *but, however*), and a conclusion.

## Verifying Spelling

**DIRECTIONS** Use an online or print dictionary to verify that all the words in the sentences below are spelled correctly. Remember that homophones, or words that sound the same but have different spellings and meanings, can often lead to spelling errors. Circle any misspelled words, and write the correct spelling on the line.

1. I finally beet my high score! _____

2. We had to weight for tickets. _____

3. Use what you learned in today's lessen to help you with the homework.

_____

Describe the steps you would take to use a dictionary to verify a word's spelling.

_____

_____

_____

 Students write routinely for a range of tasks, purposes, and audiences. Students practice various conventions of standard English.

### Endings -ed, -ing, -s

**DIRECTIONS** Use the ending *-ed, -ing,* or *-s* to change the underlined verb in each sentence to the tense indicated. On the line, rewrite the sentence with the new tense so that it makes sense. You might need to add, delete, or change the spelling of some other words.

**1.** Change to past: Uncle Steve <u>calls</u> breakfast the most important meal of the day.

_____

**2.** Change to present: He <u>has been cooking</u> eggs and spinach every morning.

_____

**3.** Change to in process: <u>I have tried</u> to get him to cook something else.

_____

**4.** Change to past: He <u>makes</u> his own favorite food every day without thinking.

_____

**5.** Change to present: Let's hope my most recent request <u>is making</u> a difference.

_____

**DIRECTIONS** Read each sentence. Then add *-s, -ed,* or *-ing* to the word in parentheses and complete the sentence correctly.

**6.** Tomorrow, I am _____ on vacation. (go)

**7.** I _____ to go last week, but my flight was cancelled. (plan)

**8.** Something always _____ in the way of my plans! (get)

**9.** I was already _____ in the taxi to the airport. (ride)

**10.** My sister _____ to tell me about the big storm. (call)

**11.** The hurricane _____ flights from landing. (prevent)

**12.** Fortunately, my hotel was not _____. (damage)

**13.** Now I will be _____ the aftermath of the storm. (witness)

**14.** The driver is just _____ up to the terminal. (pull)

**15.** I hope the plane _____ on time today! (leave)

Students apply grade-level phonics and word analysis skills.

Name _____

**DIRECTIONS** Write a sentence using each word.

illusion    indignant    destructive    persisted

_____

_____

_____

_____

_____

**Write in Response to Reading**

Do George's parents and Eric have more similarities or differences? Cite text evidence in your response. Write your response below, on a separate sheet of paper, or in a new document.

_____

_____

_____

_____

_____

Students demonstrate contextual understanding of Benchmark Vocabulary. Students read text closely and use text evidence in their written answers.

**Establish a Situation** Think about how you might introduce a narrator, characters, setting, and a conflict for your science fiction narrative. On a separate sheet of paper or in a new document, freewrite for 15 minutes. Try to write continuously, without pausing to edit or review your work. Write down all the ideas that come to your mind. You will select the best ideas at a later time.

**Conventions**

## Common and Proper Nouns

**DIRECTIONS** Underline each common noun once and each proper noun twice in the sentences below.

1. Agatha bought some boots at a store in Nashville, Tennessee.

2. Luke's mother drove him to Franklin High School so that he could watch the game.

3. Whenever Maria and Tyra go to the fair, they visit their aunt in Jackson.

4. We will read a biography of Langston Hughes and a collection of his poetry this week.

5. The twins are finishing a wreath for Mrs. Morrison's door, and they will give it to her on Saturday.

Students write routinely for a range of tasks, purposes, and audiences. Students practice various conventions of standard English.

Name _____

**DIRECTIONS** Write a sentence using each word.

offended    enlightenment    inquiry    fusion

_____

_____

_____

_____

_____

**Write in Response to Reading**

Write an explanatory paragraph about how the narrator's point of view affects the reader's interpretation of events. Choose one specific passage from the text to support your answer. Write your response below, on a separate sheet of paper, or in a new document.

_____

_____

_____

_____

Students demonstrate contextual understanding of Benchmark Vocabulary. Students read text closely and use text evidence in their written answers.

## Point of View

**DIRECTIONS** Using evidence from the text, answer the following questions about pages 40–42 from *George's Secret Key to the Universe*.

1. How does George feel about taking the oath?

   _____

   _____

2. Which details from the narrator's description of George help develop this idea?

   _____

   _____

   _____

3. How does George feel when trying to figure out which key to press on Cosmos's keyboard?

   _____

   _____

4. Which details from the narrator's description of George help develop this idea?

   _____

   _____

   _____

Students analyze and respond to literary and informational text.

**Establish a Narrator's Point of View**  On a separate sheet of paper or in a new document, add to your freewrite from Lesson 1. Use the third-person limited point of view to explain the main character's thoughts, feelings, motivations, and reasons for his or her actions.

**Conventions**

## Concrete and Abstract Nouns

**DIRECTIONS**  Underline the abstract nouns in the sentences below from pages 40–41 of *George's Secret Key to the Universe*.

"I shall be courageous and careful in my quest for greater knowledge about the mysteries that surround us. I shall not use scientific knowledge for my own personal gain or give it to those who seek to destroy the wonderful planet on which we live.

"If I break this oath, may the beauty and wonder of the Universe forever remain hidden from me."

Students write routinely for a range of tasks, purposes, and audiences. Students practice various conventions of standard English.

Name _____

**DIRECTIONS** Write a sentence using each word.

menacing     ambling     inspiration     accelerate

_____

_____

_____

_____

**Write in Response to Reading**

Choose the most effective sensory description or figurative language from Chapter 7. Use details from the text to describe why the language is so effective. Write your response below, on a separate sheet of paper, or in a new document.

_____

_____

_____

_____

_____

Students demonstrate contextual
understanding of Benchmark Vocabulary.
Students read text closely and use text
evidence in their written answers.

## Technology and Treasure

Historians estimate that about three million shipwrecks lie on the ocean floor. Many contain gold, silver, or precious gems. Why not grab a snorkel and fins, take a few diving lessons, and head into the ocean to find a treasure? Unfortunately, it's not that simple. Famous treasure hunter Mel Fisher and his crew spent sixteen years searching for the wreck of the seventeenth-century Spanish ship *Atocha* (ah-TOE-chah) before locating it in 1985.

High-tech electronic equipment has made the task of finding underwater treasure— like the more than 100,000 silver coins found in the *Atocha*—a lot easier than it once was. Consider the steps that many modern treasure hunters take.

**Find the Wreck** Sonar devices towed behind ships send out sound waves, which bounce off the ocean floor and back to the ship. A computer creates a three-dimensional map that can be used to locate hidden wrecks. Even ships completely covered by sand can be detected.

**Get to the Wreck** Divers use SCUBA (**S**elf-**C**ontained **U**nderwater **B**reathing **A**pparatus) gear to explore wrecks in shallow water. The diver, breathing a mixture of gases held in tanks, carries a light, safety equipment, and tools. In deep water, searchers operate sophisticated robotic devices, including **R**emotely **O**perated **V**ehicles (ROVs).

**Locate Buried Objects** Sand shifts with ocean currents, so divers may use submersible detectors to locate metals below the ocean floor. Other devices similar to leaf blowers move sand and sediment away from objects. Reversing the flow of air can vacuum small items directly up to the recovery ship.

**Map the Site** Divers use powerful lights and high-definition cameras to take thousands of photographs. These are assembled into a detailed map of the wreck.

**Recover Objects** Crews on recovery ships lower baskets to bring up small objects. Cranes or robotic arms move larger items. The water dredge is another useful excavation tool. With a long tube, it functions much like an underwater vacuum cleaner.

**Conserve Artifacts** Objects exposed to seawater for centuries are often covered with minerals. Conservation experts use everything from dental picks to air-powered chisels to expose the treasure underneath the crust.

All this technology is not cheap. Mel Fisher spent more than $58 million in his search for the *Atocha*. Is it worth it? Many marine treasure hunters think so. Like a buried time capsule, shipwrecks may hold valuable treasures and also provide a fascinating window into the past.

 Students read text closely to determine what the text says.

Name _____

**Gather Evidence** On page 214, underline a text detail that suggests the author's purpose for writing the selection.

**Gather Evidence: Extend Your Ideas** How does the first paragraph support the author's purpose for writing the selection? Write your answer below.

_____

**Ask Questions** Write two questions you could ask the author about how technology has changed searching for shipwrecks.

_____

_____

**Ask Questions: Extend Your Ideas** Look at the two questions you wrote. List one print and one online source you could use to find the answers to your questions.

_____

**Make Your Case** Choose two scientific vocabulary terms. Use a print or online dictionary to find the definition that best relates to how the word is used in the text. Write each word and its meaning below.

_____

_____

**Make Your Case: Extend Your Ideas** Write an original sentence for each word you chose. Discuss your sentences with a partner.

_____

_____

 Students read text closely to determine what the text says.

**Use Descriptions to Develop Characters** On a separate sheet of paper or in a new document, write a one- to two-page character sketch for the protagonist (main character) of the story you have been working on. Using descriptive details that appeal to the five sentences and figurative language, describe the character's appearance, actions, motivations, personality, and attitude. Remember that an effective description *shows* how a character feels rather than simply naming the emotion and creates a vivid picture for readers, allowing them to imagine the character in action.

**Conventions**

## Plural or Singular Nouns

**DIRECTIONS** Read the first paragraph on page 69 of *George's Secret Key to the Universe*. Write each singular, plural, and collective noun from the paragraph in the appropriate place on the chart below.

| Singular Nouns | |
|---|---|
| **Plural Nouns** | |
| **Collective Nouns** | |

Students write routinely for a range of tasks, purposes, and audiences. Students practice various conventions of standard English.

Name _____

**DIRECTIONS** Write a sentence using each word.

defiantly    improvised    spiraled    instinctively

_____

_____

_____

_____

_____

**Write in Response to Reading**

Explain how the sequence of events in Chapters 10 and 11 is presented as a series of scenes. Discuss how the chapter structure helps to organize events. Write your response below, on a separate sheet of paper, or in a new document.

_____

_____

_____

_____

_____

Students demonstrate contextual understanding of Benchmark Vocabulary. Students read text closely and use text evidence in their written answers.

Name _____

## Fitting Narrative Pieces Together

**DIRECTIONS** Using evidence from the text, answer the following questions about pages 95–98 of *George's Secret Key to the Universe*.

1. What do Annie and George land on in outer space at the beginning of Chapter 11? Why does Annie choose to take him there?

   _____

   _____

   _____

2. How does this connect to previous chapters in the text?

   _____

   _____

   _____

   _____

   _____

3. What problem does George have on page 97? Why does he have this problem?

   _____

   _____

   _____

4. How does Annie respond to George? How does this help prove her point (her reason for taking him there)?

   _____

   _____

   _____

 Students analyze and respond to literary and informational text.

**Organize Event Sequence**   On a separate sheet of paper or in a new document, use a Story Sequence B graphic organizer to plan a series of main events that include elements of science fiction. Then create a series of scenes that happen during each main event. Scenes may include dialogue, a description of a new setting, an action sequence, a flashback, or background information. Finally, use this information to add to your narrative. Be sure to include appropriate transitions and time-order words to show the sequence of events.

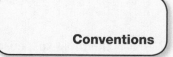

**Conventions**

## Pronouns

**DIRECTIONS**   Reread page 92 of *George's Secret Key to the Universe*. List each pronoun you find on the page in the appropriate column.

| Personal | Possessive | Relative | Indefinite |
|----------|-----------|----------|-----------|
|          |           |          |           |
|          |           |          |           |
|          |           |          |           |
|          |           |          |           |
|          |           |          |           |
|          |           |          |           |
|          |           |          |           |

Students write routinely for a range of tasks, purposes, and audiences. Students practice various conventions of standard English.

**DIRECTIONS** Write a sentence using each word.

massive    divert    summon    device

_____

_____

_____

_____

_____

**Write in Response to Reading**

What is the most suspenseful moment from Chapters 12–14? Explain your answer using evidence from the text. Write your answer below, on a separate sheet of a paper, or in a new document.

_____

_____

_____

_____

_____

Students demonstrate contextual understanding of Benchmark Vocabulary. Students read text closely and use text evidence in their written answers.

**Use Pacing to Develop Events**  On a separate sheet of paper or in a new document, build on your science fiction narrative by developing the rising action. Focus on pacing to slow down and speed up action as you add new events to develop the story, introduce a series of smaller conflicts leading up to the main conflict, and develop the characters' responses to new situations. Be sure to use language and pacing that builds suspense and tension.

**Conventions**

## Personal Pronouns

**DIRECTIONS**  Underline the personal pronoun that serves as the subject of the sentence, and circle the personal pronoun(s) that serves as an object in the sentence.

1. But then he spotted a small chunk of rock calmly floating next to him.

2. She looked under the bed but could not find them.

3. We go to Boston every year and never take him with us.

4. You can ride a bike across it in just five minutes.

5. Will they help her move the boxes tomorrow?

Students write routinely for a range of tasks, purposes, and audiences. Students practice various conventions of standard English.

## Suffixes -ly, -ian

**DIRECTIONS** On the line, write the word from the Word Bank that matches each definition.

### Word Bank

| | | | | |
|---|---|---|---|---|
| politician | outwardly | secretly | historian | physician |
| mercifully | antiquarian | calmly | civilian | unfortunately |
| roughly | inventively | pedestrian | solidly | |

1. without any doubt _____

2. slowly and confidently _____

3. a person who is walking _____

4. as far as others can see _____

5. not as good as was hoped _____

6. person who studies the past _____

7. with sympathetic kindness _____

8. hidden from view _____

9. person who enjoys old objects _____

10. a nonmilitary member of society _____

11. with a lack of care or precision _____

12. person who treats sick people _____

13. person who runs for office _____

14. with originality _____

**DIRECTIONS** Add -ly or -ian to the underlined word to complete the sentence. Write the full word on the line.

15. _____ He ordered new glasses from the optic.

16. _____ The final score was high unusual.

17. _____ Sad, our school's team lost the debate.

18. _____ You would have to be a magic to fix that!

19. _____ The water level is impressive high.

 Students apply grade-level phonics and word analysis skills.

Name _____

**DIRECTIONS** Write a sentence using each word.

uninhabitable    havoc    ominously    deliberately

_____

_____

_____

_____

_____

_____

**Write in Response to Reading**

Explain how punctuation and style create natural-sounding speech in dialogue. Include text evidence and page numbers in your response. Write your response below, on a separate sheet of paper, or in a new document.

_____

_____

_____

_____

_____

_____

Students demonstrate contextual understanding of Benchmark Vocabulary. Students read text closely and use text evidence in their written answers.

**Develop Dialogue**  On a separate sheet of paper or in a new document, add dialogue to the narrative you have been working on.  Focus on two or three paragraphs, and use natural-sounding dialogue to develop main characters, illustrate characters' responses to events, and develop main events. Be sure to capitalize the appropriate words and use quotation marks and other punctuation correctly.

**Conventions**

## Possessive Pronouns

**DIRECTIONS**  Underline the possessive pronoun(s) in each sentence.

1.  Annie pulled off her heavy space boots and spacesuit.

2.  "Yeah, but you're not allowed in my kitchen, are you?"

3.  This copy of the book must be yours because I accidentally ripped the cover of my book.

4.  Whenever he feels sick, he makes an appointment with his doctor.

5.  The car will be ours if we can guess its price.

 Students write routinely for a range of tasks, purposes, and audiences. Students practice various conventions of standard English.

**Suffix** *-ize*

**DIRECTIONS** Read the paragraph. Circle each word that contains the suffix *-ize*. Write those words to the left of the numbers below. On the right, write a new sentence that contains the word.

Ms. Dobbs needed workers who specialize in carpentry. It took time for the thought to crystallize that we could do the work. We can customize bookcases to minimize the space they occupy while we maximize their capacity. We can accessorize the bookcases with fancy handles. Because Ms. Dobbs wants to downsize, she seized on our idea. In the next few days, we will formalize our proposal so she can authorize us to begin work.

_____ 1. _____

_____ 2. _____

_____ 3. _____

_____ 4. _____

_____ 5. _____

_____ 6. _____

_____ 7. _____

_____ 8. _____

**DIRECTIONS** Add the suffix *-ize* to the word in parentheses to complete the sentence. Change the spelling of the base word if necessary.

9. To sound good, we must (harmony). _____

10. Darcy likes to (drama) simple disagreements. _____

11. He was worried that someone would (burglar) his car. _____

12. With a small engine, we can (motor) that bike. _____

13. I can (sympathy) with people who feel sad. _____

14. The word will stand out more if you (italic) it. _____

15. We go to puppy play group so the dogs can (social). _____

Students apply grade-level phonics and word analysis skills.

Name _____

**DIRECTIONS** Write a sentence using each word.

emits     intrigued     emerged

_____

_____

_____

_____

**Write in Response to Reading**

Does George respond well to conflict? Use details from Chapter 19 to support your response. Write your answer below, on a separate sheet of paper, or in a new document.

_____

_____

_____

_____

_____

Students demonstrate contextual understanding of Benchmark Vocabulary. Students read text closely and use text evidence in their written answers.

**Develop Conflict** Develop internal conflict, external conflict, or both in your story by adding events that create rising action and lead to the climax of the story. Be sure to develop the characters' interactions around science fiction topics, situations, or events. Use a separate sheet of paper or start a new document.

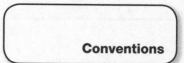

**Conventions**

## Proper Case for Pronouns

**DIRECTIONS** Reread page 177 of *George's Secret Key to the Universe*. Write each subjective, objective, and possessive pronoun in the appropriate row below.

| | |
|---|---|
| **Subjective Pronouns** | |
| **Objective Pronouns** | |
| **Possessive Pronouns** | |

Students write routinely for a range of tasks, purposes, and audiences. Students practice various conventions of standard English.

Name _____

**DIRECTIONS** Write a sentence using each word.

advocate    alter    fundamental    vital

_____

_____

_____

_____

_____

_____

**Write in Response to Reading**

Write a paragraph about the mood created by two different settings in *George's Secret Key to the Universe*. Develop the topic with details or quotations from the text. Use linking words to show relationships between ideas, such as *in contrast or similarly*. Write your response below, on a separate sheet of paper, or in a new document.

_____

_____

_____

_____

_____

_____

Students demonstrate contextual understanding of Benchmark Vocabulary. Students read text closely and use text evidence in their written answers.

Name _____

## Comparing and Contrasting Settings

**DIRECTIONS** Using evidence from the text, answer the following questions about pages 179–182 from *George's Secret Key to the Universe*.

1. What is the setting on pages 179–180?

   _____

2. What details help develop the setting on pages 179–180?

   _____

   _____

   _____

   _____

3. What is the setting of the rest of Chapter 20?

   _____

4. What details help develop the setting on page 182?

   _____

   _____

   _____

   _____

5. How are these settings alike or different?

   _____

   _____

6. How are they alike or different in affecting the story's mood?

   _____

   _____

Students analyze and respond to literary and informational text.

**Develop Setting**   Choose an event from the sequence drafted in Lesson 4, and visualize the setting for that event.  On a separate sheet of paper or in a new document, write a detailed description of the setting using precise details to describe the time and place.

**Conventions**

### Relative Pronouns

**DIRECTIONS**  Write the relative pronoun *that, which, who,* or *whose* to correctly complete each sentence.

1. George met with his teacher, _____ gave him an assignment.

2. The iron bar became oxidized, _____ means "rusted."

3. Eric read the note _____ contained misinformation.

4. The professor _____ thinks there is life on Mars loves to talk about it.

5. Dr. Reeper, _____ handwriting George recognized, was trying to trap Eric.

Students write routinely for a range of tasks, purposes, and audiences. Students practice various conventions of standard English.

Name _____

**DIRECTIONS** Write a sentence using each word.

objected     distorted     erratically     engulf

_____

_____

_____

_____

_____

_____

**Write in Response to Reading**

What is the most effective visual element in Chapters 23–25? Use details from the text to support your response. Write your response below, on a separate sheet of paper, or in a new document.

_____

_____

_____

_____

_____

_____

Students demonstrate contextual understanding of Benchmark Vocabulary. Students read text closely and use text evidence in their written answers.

Name _____

**Develop Theme and Resolve Events**  On a separate sheet of paper or in a new document, complete your story by revising it and adding a two- to three-paragraph ending that resolves the action and conveys the theme.  Focus on showing your characters' responses to the situation, as well as how they respond to and resolve the conflict.

**Conventions**

## Indefinite Pronouns

**DIRECTIONS**  Circle the indefinite pronoun in each sentence, and write whether it is singular or plural.

1.  Most of the screen was full of stars. _____

2.  Some of the books in Eric's library were in French. _____

3.  Whenever we go to the museum, someone gets lost. _____

4.  Anyone can try out for the basketball team. _____

5.  My father reminds me that few know how to build an engine. _____

 Students write routinely for a range of tasks, purposes, and audiences. Students practice various conventions of standard English.

## Lesson 10

Name _____

**DIRECTIONS** Write a sentence using each word.

ultimate     galaxy     remnants     perplexed

_____

_____

_____

_____

_____

_____

**Write in Response to Reading**

Look at the illustrations in Chapters 26–28 of *George's Secret Key to the Universe*. Choose one illustration, and explain how it helps you understand the text. Write your response below, on a separate sheet of paper, or in a new document.

_____

_____

_____

_____

_____

_____

Students demonstrate contextual understanding of Benchmark Vocabulary. Students read text closely and use text evidence in their written answers.

## Text Structure and Visual Elements

**DIRECTIONS**  Using evidence from the text, answer the following questions about Chapters 26–28 of *George's Secret Key to the Universe*.

**1.** How is the text in Chapter 26 structured?

_____

_____

_____

**2.** How does the sidebar (pages 234–235) enhance the information in Eric's book?

_____

_____

_____

_____

**3.** How is the text in Chapters 27 and 28 structured?

_____

_____

_____

**4.** How do the illustrations in Chapters 27 and 28 add to the story's plot? Use specific examples from the text.

_____

_____

_____

_____

Students analyze and respond to literary and informational text.

**Develop a Scene**  On a separate sheet of paper or in a new document, write a two-page scene based on a topic featured in *George's Secret Key to the Universe*. Introduce an event and use descriptive details and dialogue to develop this event over the course of the scene. Refer to your answers from the Prepare to Write section and use this information to think about how to establish a situation to orient the reader.

**Conventions**

## Intensive Pronouns

**DIRECTIONS**  Underline the intensive pronoun in each sentence.

1. Annie decided to talk to George herself and clear up his confusion.

2. The pig shook itself and dashed through the open pigsty door; George himself was to blame for leaving the door open.

3. Michael hurt himself sliding across the court, but he could not bandage the wound himself.

4. Wanda and Fletcher would have done it themselves if they had been given enough time.

5. I finished the report myself, so I know it includes the results from all of our experiments.

 Students write routinely for a range of tasks, purposes, and audiences. Students practice various conventions of standard English.

## Prefixes *com-, epi-, pro-*

**DIRECTIONS** Refer to the definitions of the prefixes *com-, epi-,* and *pro-*. Add one of the prefixes to a word from the Word Bank to complete each sentence.

*com-* with, together, thoroughly
*epi-* on, at, before, after
*pro-* before, forward, forth, for

### Word Bank

| | | | |
|---|---|---|---|
| test | long | fort | press |
| graph | portion | pound | center |

1. The oversized couch is not in _____ to the small room.

2. She had to _____ her hour-long speech into ten minutes!

3. The _____ preceding Chapter 1 set the tone of the book.

4. The marchers were part of a _____ movement.

5. I hope they do not _____ this boring play much longer.

6. Dad used warm milk to _____ the baby.

7. Lydia located the _____ of the earthquake on the map.

8. Detectives sent the mysterious _____ to the lab for testing.

**DIRECTIONS** Read the meaning of each root. Add the prefix shown, write the word, and write a possible definition of the new word.

9. *bust,* to burn, + *com-* = _____

   Definition: _____

10. *voke,* voice or call, + *pro-* = _____

    Definition: _____

11. *pose,* place, + *com-* = _____

    Definition: _____

12. *trude,* push or thrust, + *pro-* = _____

    Definition: _____

 Students apply grade-level phonics and word analysis skills.

Name _____

**DIRECTIONS** Write a sentence using each word.

accessing      exploiting      agitated

_____

_____

_____

_____

**Write in Response to Reading**

Read the last two pages of Chapter 30. Then give your opinion as to whether Eric should try to make up with Dr. Reeper. Use evidence from the text in your response. Write your response below, on a separate sheet of paper, or in a new document.

_____

_____

_____

_____

_____

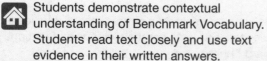
Students demonstrate contextual understanding of Benchmark Vocabulary. Students read text closely and use text evidence in their written answers.

**Expand and Revise a Draft** Review the scene you wrote in Lesson 10 and identify key events in the scene. Then think about how each character might react to those events and expand and revise your draft on a separate sheet of paper. Be sure to use precise words as well as figurative language, such as similes and metaphors, to describe your characters' reactions. Remember to also include sensory details as you develop important character reactions.

**Conventions**

## Pronoun-Antecedent Agreement

**DIRECTIONS** Complete each sentence with the correct pronoun.

1. Michael and Tristan were best friends in second grade, but now _____ do not talk to each other.

2. Annie heard _____ mother and father speaking quietly.

3. My sister and I took _____ dog with us to the park.

4. Louis cannot fix the car, so _____ will have to take it to a mechanic.

5. Most of the students have turned in _____ assignments early.

Students write routinely for a range of tasks, purposes, and audiences. Students practice various conventions of standard English.

**DIRECTIONS** Write a sentence using each word.

vigorous    commotion

_____

_____

_____

_____

**Write in Response to Reading**

Read the last sentence on page 286. Explain how the information adds to the chapter and to the text as a whole. What does it add to the theme of the novel? Use text evidence to support your response. Write your response below, on a separate sheet of paper, or in a new document.

_____

_____

_____

_____

_____

_____

Students demonstrate contextual understanding of Benchmark Vocabulary. Students read text closely and use text evidence in their written answers.

**Plan a Science Fiction Narrative**  Plan an original science fiction narrative based on something you learned from *George's Secret Key to the Universe*. Think about the purpose (to entertain) and determine the audience for your narrative. Then, on a separate sheet of paper or in a new document, use a Story Sequence B graphic organizer to develop its characters, setting, and events.

**Conventions**

## Pronoun-Antecedent Agreement

**DIRECTIONS**  Rewrite each sentence below so that the pronoun and its antecedent agree. There is more than one way to correct each sentence.

1. Each of the teachers brought their plans to the meeting. _____

   _____

2. Everyone in the class had their notes at the assembly. _____

   _____

3. Somebody can eat their lunch at my desk. _____

   _____

4. Neither of the boys can take the game with them to school. _____

   _____

5. Nobody wants their prize taken away. _____

   _____

 Students write routinely for a range of tasks, purposes, and audiences. Students practice various conventions of standard English.

Name _____

**DIRECTIONS** Write a sentence using each word.

lunar     horizon     vessel

_____

_____

_____

_____

**Write in Response to Reading**

Read the second paragraph on page 6. Use details from the passage to write an informative paragraph explaining conditions on the surface of the moon. Write your response below, on a separate sheet of paper, or in a new document.

_____

_____

_____

_____

_____

_____

Students demonstrate contextual understanding of Benchmark Vocabulary. Students read text closely and use text evidence in their written answers.

## Careers in the Space Industry

Do you like gazing at the stars on a clear night? Are you fascinated by the enormity of the universe? Do you wonder if there is life "out there"? Perhaps a career in the space industry is for you. Most of the job opportunities in space exploration or research involve science and math, but writers and artists also play a role in this exciting field.

The most common career involving space is astronomy. Astronomers use science to study the universe. These men and women study the motions, positions, sizes, and makeup of heavenly bodies, such as stars, planets, and galaxies. Astronomers often get their doctoral degrees. Their jobs might involve teaching at a university, doing research about how something in space works, or using enormous telescopes and supercomputers to analyze how objects in space move.

Some astronomers specialize in astrophysics. That is, they study the physical and chemical measurements of heavenly bodies. The astrophysicists at the National Aeronautics and Space Administration (NASA) focus on answering three main questions: How does the universe work? How did we get here? Are we alone? These specialists use their knowledge of physics, along with advanced technology, to continue to search for answers to these questions.

If this kind of science isn't up your alley, you might be interested in another career in the space industry—engineering. Electrical engineers are responsible for designing rocket engines, propulsion devices, and satellites. They focus on the way these things will function outside Earth's atmosphere. Mechanical engineers work on any moving parts of a spacecraft, from radios to robots. They, too, have to think about the way the space environment will affect materials. Finally, software engineers program the computers that run the spacecraft that electrical and mechanical engineers design.

If your skills are more focused in the arts, you will be happy to learn that the space industry also caters to your talents. Universities, private corporations, and government agencies all need writers to share their visions and their progress with the public. Artists might collaborate with writers to illustrate the explanations of how spacecraft work, for example.

Even if the space industry does not include the right career for you, you can still enjoy gazing at the night sky on a clear evening.

 Students read text closely to determine what the text says.

**Gather Evidence** Underline three objects that electrical engineers design. Circle three things that astronomers study.

**Gather Evidence: Extend Your Ideas** What would an electrical engineer do with a satellite? What would an astronomer do with a satellite?

_____

_____

**Ask Questions** Write two questions about careers in the space industry that begin with *where*.

_____

_____

**Ask Questions: Extend Your Ideas** Write two questions about careers in the space industry that begin with *how*.

_____

_____

**Make Your Case** Select one career mentioned in the passage, and use a detail from the text to explain why it would be a satisfying or rewarding career.

_____

_____

**Make Your Case: Extend Your Ideas** Choose the career mentioned in the passage that you find most interesting. List some steps you could take to prepare yourself for that career. Discuss your result with a partner.

_____

_____

Students read text closely to determine what the text says.

**Draft Science Fiction** Using your Story Sequence B graphic organizer from Lesson 12, draft two to three pages of your science fiction narrative on separate sheets of paper or in a new document. Think about your purpose (to entertain), and determine your audience. Then develop your characters and create well-organized events. Be sure to include science fiction elements, such as futuristic or imagined characters, settings, and/or events, and add dialogue to help develop characters and events.

**Conventions**

### Linking Verbs

**DIRECTIONS** Underline the linking verbs in each sentence. Then draw a box around its subject, and circle the word or words that rename or describe that subject.

1. Neil and Buzz seemed  happy  after they conducted experiments on the moon.

2. William felt  guilty  about not returning the library book on time.

3. Laila was  worried  about performing in front of an audience.

4. Even though she is a  musician, she rarely plays in concerts.

5. When my mother comes home from work, she always looks  exhausted.

Students write routinely for a range of tasks, purposes, and audiences. Students practice various conventions of standard English.

**DIRECTIONS** Write a sentence using each word.

atmosphere     potentially     quarantine     facility

_____

_____

_____

_____

_____

**Write in Response to Reading**

Consider Michael Collins's decision to never travel in space again. Do you agree or disagree with his decision? Support your answer using cause-effect relationships from the text. Write your response below, on a separate sheet of paper, or in a new document.

_____

_____

_____

_____

_____

Students demonstrate contextual understanding of Benchmark Vocabulary. Students read text closely and use text evidence in their written answers.

## Cause-Effect Relationships

**DIRECTIONS** Using evidence from the text, answer the following questions about pages 12–17 from *The Man Who Went to the Far Side of the Moon*.

1. On page 12, how does weightlessness in space affect the way astronauts eat food?

   _____

   _____

   _____

   _____

   _____

2. On page 14, what results from the mice surviving in the quarantine trailer with the astronauts? Why does this occur?

   _____

   _____

3. On page 15, why are there scientific experiments, television cameras and cables, Hasselblad cameras, and empty food packages still on the moon?

   _____

   _____

4. On page 17, why does Collins feel lucky to live on Earth?

   _____

   _____

   _____

Students analyze and respond to literary and informational text.

Name _____

**Revise or Rewrite Science Fiction** Exchange your science fiction narrative with a partner. As you review your partner's draft, consider the following questions:

1. Does the organization and sequence make sense? Are there transitions?

2. Are there vague or general words that should be replaced with more concrete words?

3. Does the dialogue sound natural?

4. Is the sentence structure effective, and does it vary throughout?

Using the feedback from your partner, revise or rewrite your narrative on separate sheets of paper or in a new document. Add transitions to clarify organization; develop characters by elaborating with concrete details, sensory details, and stronger word choice; use fragments and slang to make dialogue more realistic; and combine, expand, or reduce sentences to vary structure.

**Conventions**

**Linking Verbs**

**DIRECTIONS** Write *A* if the underlined verb is used as an action verb or *L* if it is used as a linking verb.

1. Michael thought the freeze-dried shrimp cocktail <u>tasted</u> great. _____

2. He <u>tasted</u> the fruit cocktail and did not like it _____

3. Luella <u>grew</u> tomatoes and cucumbers in her garden. _____

4. When the plantains <u>smelled</u> sweet, they were ripe enough to cook. _____

5. Kyrie could <u>smell</u> the flowers on the table from his bedroom. _____

Students write routinely for a range of tasks, purposes, and audiences. Students practice various conventions of standard English.

**DIRECTIONS** Write a sentence using each word.

illusion     vigorous     atmosphere     potentially

_____

_____

_____

_____

_____

**Write in Response to Reading**

Write a paragraph that explains the traits an astronaut needs. Use evidence from both texts in your response. Write your response below, on a separate sheet of paper, or in a new document.

_____

_____

_____

_____

_____

_____

 Students demonstrate contextual understanding of Benchmark Vocabulary. Students read text closely and use text evidence in their written answers.

Name _____

## Compare and Contrast Characters

**DIRECTIONS** Using evidence from the texts, answer the following questions about *George's Secret Key to the Universe* and *The Man Who Went to the Far Side of the Moon.*

1. How are Eric's and Michael's attitudes about their work exploring space similar?

   _____

   _____

2. How are Eric's and Michael's attitudes about their work exploring space different?

   _____

   _____

   _____

3. How are Eric's and Michael's views about Earth similar and different?

   _____

   _____

   _____

4. How are Eric's and Michael's views about family similar or different?

   _____

   _____

   _____

Students analyze and respond to literary and informational text.

**Edit and Proofread Science Fiction** Find a new partner and exchange revised drafts of your science fiction narratives. Use the checklist below to review your partner's narrative for correct grammar, punctuation, spelling, and use of pronouns.

- ☐ All proper nouns are capitalized.
- ☐ All dialogue is correctly punctuated.
- ☐ All words are spelled correctly.
- ☐ Narration uses complete sentences.
- ☐ Pronouns are used correctly.

**Conventions**

## Verb Phrases

**DIRECTIONS** Underline the verb phrase(s) in each sentence. Then circle the helping verb(s).

1. I am traveling to San Francisco by train.

2. The Flemings should adopt another dog.

3. She has been writing this book for over six months now.

4. Nancy and Isabelle will visit their aunt during the holiday break.

5. Jeremiah must finish his chores before he can play basketball with his friends.

 Students write routinely for a range of tasks, purposes, and audiences. Students practice various conventions of standard English.

## Idioms

**DIRECTIONS** Read the paragraph below. Using your knowledge of the ordinary meanings of words, decide which underlined phrases are idioms. Then use context clues and print or digital resources to determine the meaning of the idioms. Write the idioms and their meanings on the lines.

Lan had <u>performed flawlessly.</u> The <u>curtains parted</u> for her bow. Suddenly, Alvin leapt onto the stage. He completely <u>stole her thunder!</u> The audience kept applauding, but Lan gestured to the stagehands to <u>pull the plug</u> on the curtain call. To <u>add insult to injury,</u> Alvin grabbed her arm. The <u>applause quieted.</u> Alvin held her hand and knelt down. "This is <u>the last straw!</u>" Lan hissed. Alvin knew he was <u>going out on a limb.</u> "Marry me, Lan," he whispered, "and I will love you <u>till the cows come home.</u>"

**1.** _____

Definition: _____

**2.** _____

Definition: _____

**3.** _____

Definition: _____

**4.** _____

Definition: _____

**5.** _____

Definition: _____

**6.** _____

Definition: _____

Students apply grade-level phonics and word analysis skills.

**DIRECTIONS** Write a sentence using each word.

mayday        manual        radiation

_____

_____

_____

_____

**Write in Response to Reading**

Use details from the text to write an opinion paragraph explaining whether you would like or dislike traveling to Mars with Justin and Alicia as your fellow pilots. Write your response below, on a separate sheet of paper, or in a new document.

_____

_____

_____

_____

_____

Students demonstrate contextual understanding of Benchmark Vocabulary. Students read text closely and use text evidence in their written answers.

Name _____

**Publish and Present Science Fiction** Prepare to present the science fiction narrative you created in Lessons 12–15. Cut out photos, graphs, maps, charts, and other visuals that you can use in a presentation about your narrative, and create layouts by hand. Focus on presenting main ideas and interesting points from your story, including information about the characters and key events. Then annotate your narrative in order to decide how to adjust rate and expression to reflect emotion and intensity in your narrative.

**Conventions**

### Linking Verb or Helping Verb

**DIRECTIONS** Read each sentence carefully. Then underline the form of the verb *be* that serves as a linking verb, and circle the form of the verb *be* that serves as a helping verb.

1. "I am the captain of this space pod, and we are going to crash!"

2. She was calling "Mayday" for help, but she was calm.

3. Moira will be watching the game tonight, but Frank is too tired to join her.

4. We were frustrated because the mover was driving so slowly.

5. The plane is flying over the Grand Canyon, but Wesley is scared and will not look out of the window.

Students write routinely for a range of tasks, purposes, and audiences. Students practice various conventions of standard English.

**DIRECTIONS** Write a sentence using each word.

enlightenment    inquiry    vital    mayday

_____

_____

_____

_____

_____

**Write in Response to Reading**

Choose a theme common to both texts. Choose one character from each text, and compare and contrast how the two characters help develop the theme in their respective texts. Include each character's attitude toward the theme, as well as the characters' responses to actions or events that help develop the theme. Write your response below, on a separate sheet of paper, or in a new document.

_____

_____

_____

_____

_____

Students demonstrate contextual understanding of Benchmark Vocabulary. Students read text closely and use text evidence in their written answers.

**Compare and Contrast Themes**

**DIRECTIONS** Using evidence from the texts, answer the following questions about *George's Secret Key to the Universe* and "Mayday on Moon of Jupiter."

1. What are some key events that occur in Chapters 30–32 of *George's Secret Key to the Universe?*

   _____

   _____

   _____

   _____

2. What are some key events that occur in "Mayday on Moon of Jupiter"?

   _____

   _____

   _____

3. How do the characters' actions develop the theme(s) of each text?

   _____

   _____

   _____

   _____

4. What theme(s) do the two texts share?

   _____

   _____

   _____

   _____

Students analyze and respond to literary and informational text.

Name _____

**Conduct Research to Explore Theme** Conduct print and digital research about a real person you read about in the unit who has turned his or her curiosity about space into a career related to space exploration. Focus your research on the theme (curiosity and space exploration). Write notes on the sources you find on separate sheets of paper or in a new document. Be sure to do the following:

1. Find at least three sources, including both primary and secondary sources.

2. Paraphrase, summarize, and quote directly to take notes on your sources.

3. Cite correct source information.

**Conventions**

## Principal Parts of Regular Verbs

**DIRECTIONS** On the line next to each sentence, identify whether the underlined verb is the present tense, present participle, past tense, or past participle form of a regular verb.

1. She <u>said</u> that she would bring the keys tonight. _____

2. Morgan and Betty are <u>walking</u> down the block. _____

3. The group has <u>filed</u> a petition to change the ordinance. _____

4. Lillian is <u>working</u> on an important report this week. _____

5. Christopher <u>likes</u> his new home and his new school. _____

Students write routinely for a range of tasks, purposes, and audiences. Students practice various conventions of standard English.

Name _____

**DIRECTIONS** Write a sentence using each word.

instinctively     atmosphere     potentially     radiation

_____

_____

_____

_____

_____

_____

**Write in Response to Reading**

Unlike "Mayday on Moon of Jupiter," the rising action in *George's Secret Key to the Universe* develops over the course of several chapters. Because of this, the pacing is different in the two texts. Which text was more exciting to read? Why was the text you selected more exciting to read? Explain your answer using evidence from both texts. Write your response below, on a separate sheet of paper, or in a new document.

_____

_____

_____

_____

_____

Students demonstrate contextual understanding of Benchmark Vocabulary. Students read text closely and use text evidence in their written answers.

Name _____

**Use Research to Explore Theme**  Use your research about a person involved in space exploration to write a one-page fictional journal entry from that person's perspective about the importance of curiosity in space exploration. Use details, facts, examples, and other information from your research to make the journal entry as vivid and authentic as possible. Write the journal entry on a separate sheet of paper or start a new document.

**Conventions**

## Principal Parts of Irregular Verbs

**DIRECTIONS**  Complete each sentence with the correct form of the irregular verb.

1.  As Justin _____ (*fly,* present tense) the aircraft, Alicia reads the mission manual.

2.  After the science competition ended, Susan _____ (*drive,* past tense) George and his new computer home.

3.  George discovered that the boys had _____ (*steal,* past participle) Cosmos for Dr. Reeper.

4.  When George _____ (*go,* past tense) to Eric's house, there were scientists in Eric's library.

5.  Annie had _____ (*become,* past participle) angry, and she was determined to prove to George that she was telling the truth.

 Students write routinely for a range of tasks, purposes, and audiences. Students practice various conventions of standard English.

**Synonyms**

**DIRECTIONS** From the Word Bank, choose a synonym for each underlined word. Write the synonym on the line.

**Word Bank**

| | | | | |
|---|---|---|---|---|
| muttered | extraordinary | rehearsal | amused | ability |
| meal | squeaky-clean | occasion | weighty | playing |
| parading | responded | preferred | immediately | correct |

_____ **1.** Jonas sat in class, daydreaming about his <u>lunch.</u>

_____ **2.** The sandwich had meatloaf, his <u>favorite</u> leftover.

_____ **3.** Because of band <u>practice</u>, he had missed breakfast.

_____ **4.** Playing the tuba took a lot of <u>skill</u>.

_____ **5.** It also demanded an <u>astonishing</u> amount of energy!

_____ **6.** Just imagine, Jonas thought, <u>marching</u> with a tuba.

_____ **7.** The band would be <u>performing</u> at Friday's game.

_____ **8.** Band members had <u>spotless</u> new uniforms.

_____ **9.** The <u>event</u> promised to be a feast for the eyes and ears.

_____ **10.** "Is that <u>right</u>, Jonas?" the teacher asked.

_____ **11.** Jonas sat up <u>abruptly</u> and blinked his eyes

_____ **12.** Had he <u>murmured</u>, or had he missed a question?

_____ **13.** "Are tubas incredibly <u>heavy</u>?" the teacher clarified.

_____ **14.** "Not for someone like me!" Jonas <u>replied</u>.

_____ **15.** "That's a relief," said the teacher, <u>smiling</u>.

 Students apply grade-level phonics and word analysis skills.

**Benchmark Vocabulary**

**DIRECTIONS** Write a sentence using each word.

allergic    embarrassing    cultures    stern

_____

_____

_____

_____

_____

_____

**Write in Response to Reading**

Based on details in pages 4–9, what can you infer about Jess and Layla's friendship? Use evidence from the text to support your response. Write your response below, on a separate sheet of paper, or in a new document.

_____

_____

_____

_____

_____

_____

Students demonstrate contextual understanding of Benchmark Vocabulary. Students read text closely and use text evidence in their written answers.

Name _____

**Choose and Introduce a Topic** Write one or two paragraphs that introduce a topic related to an important historical discovery about a part of our solar system. Your topic should be clear, and your introduction should interest the reader and help tell what the rest of your writing will be about. Write your paragraph(s) on a separate sheet of paper or in a new document.

**Conventions**

## Verb Tense: Simple Tenses

**DIRECTIONS** Circle the verb in each sentence. On the line next to each sentence, write *PR* if the verb is in the present tense, *PA* if the verb is in the past tense, or *F* if the verb is in the future tense.

1. The particles clumped together into masses called planetesimals. _____

2. Our weather and climate depend on the sun. _____

3. Suzanne purchased a hat for each of her grandchildren. _____

4. Alisha will bike to work for the entire week. _____

5. Dorian will invite a few of his coworkers to his birthday party. _____

Students write routinely for a range of tasks, purposes, and audiences. Students practice various conventions of standard English.

Name _____

**DIRECTIONS** Write a sentence using each word.

interactive    obvious    theories

_____

_____

_____

_____

**Write in Response to Reading**

Reread pages 11–14 of *Jess and Layla's Astronomical Assignment,* and write a paragraph that compares and contrasts the students in Dr. Goggles's classroom. Use evidence from the text in your response. Write your response below, on a separate sheet of paper, or in a new document.

_____

_____

_____

_____

_____

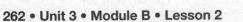
Students demonstrate contextual understanding of Benchmark Vocabulary. Students read text closely and use text evidence in their written answers.

## Compare and Contrast Characters

**DIRECTIONS** Using evidence from the text, answer the following questions about pages 10–14 from *Jess and Layla's Astronomical Assignment.*

1. How is Layla similar to her classmates Danny Phillips and Jade Jefferson?

   _____

   _____

2. Which details from the text support your answer?

   _____

   _____

   _____

   _____

3. How are Jess and Dr. Goggles similar?

   _____

   _____

   _____

4. Which details from the text support your answer?

   _____

   _____

   _____

   _____

Students analyze and respond to literary and informational text.

**Organize Ideas** On a separate sheet of paper or in a new document, create an outline or plan for your writing that develops two or three main ideas about your topic from Lesson 1. Research to find ideas and details to add to the main ideas in your outline or plan.

**Conventions**

## Verb Tense: Simple Tenses

**DIRECTIONS** For each verb below, write one sentence that uses the verb in the present tense, one that uses the verb in the past tense, and one that uses the verb in the future tense.

1. crash _____

_____

_____

_____

2. stop _____

_____

_____

_____

Students write routinely for a range of tasks, purposes, and audiences. Students practice various conventions of standard English.

**DIRECTIONS** Write a sentence using each word.

inspiration      disbelief

_____

_____

_____

_____

**Write in Response to Reading**

Reread paragraph 6 on page 20, which describes the meteors that Jess and Layla see. How does the author's word choice help you understand the event? Use specific examples from the text in your response. Write your response below, on a separate sheet of paper, or in a new document.

_____

_____

_____

_____

_____

Students demonstrate contextual understanding of Benchmark Vocabulary. Students read text closely and use text evidence in their written answers.

## Charlotte's Space Travel

Charlotte loved when her uncle visited. Uncle Ty was an engineer who worked for NASA (National Aeronautics and Space Administration). He told great stories about the rockets he helped design, and he often brought Charlotte books filled with beautiful photographs taken from space. She loved technology and science, and she was fairly adventurous. For those reasons, her family kept telling Charlotte she should be an astronaut when she grew up, but she just wasn't sure.

One Saturday, Charlotte and Uncle Ty took a trip to the city. They spent the day at the Museum of Natural History, which was hosting an exhibit on space travel. Uncle Ty provided a running narrative about various spacecraft and added interesting facts about the display of space suits and other astronaut gear. Charlotte was thrilled to try operating two model robot arms. These devices fascinated her.

By the time they got on the bus to return home, Charlotte was exhausted. Closing her eyes, she thought about what it would be like to zoom into space. As she drifted off to sleep, Charlotte started to feel the weightlessness astronauts must feel when they float in zero gravity. The next thing she knew, she was looking out the window not of a bus but of a space shuttle. She could see the vivid colors of Earth—brilliant blues and greens like she had never before witnessed.

Just then, one of her crew members floated over and nudged Charlotte, telling her she had to finish the task at hand quickly. Charlotte realized that she was maneuvering a giant robotic arm outside the space shuttle to tighten a loose panel. The pressure was on, and she felt nervous. But she kept at it. Soon enough the whole crew was celebrating Charlotte's success.

After a snack of granola, dried fruit, and nuts, the crew hooked their sleeping bags to the wall. They settled in for a good night's sleep after a long day. Charlotte dozed off, feeling proud of her accomplishment with the robotic arm and excited for the experiments they would set up the next day.

She felt like she had barely slept when all of a sudden she heard Uncle Ty's voice. "Wake up, Char," Uncle Ty whispered. "We're back home now." When Charlotte opened her eyes, she realized she had been dreaming, but this she knew for sure—she wanted to be an astronaut one day and couldn't wait for her first trip into space.

Students read text closely to determine what the text says.

**Gather Evidence** Underline Charlotte's character traits that suggest to her family why she should be an astronaut.

**Gather Evidence: Extend Your Ideas** Circle the actions in the second paragraph that connect to the personality traits that you underlined.

**Ask Questions** Write two questions you would ask the author about elements of Charlotte's dream.

_____

_____

**Ask Questions: Extend Your Ideas** Write an additional question about the dream that is answered in the text. Underline the answer in the text.

_____

_____

**Make Your Case** List character traits and actions for Uncle Ty. Compare these with Charlotte's traits and actions that you underlined and circled earlier.

_____

_____

_____

**Make Your Case: Extend Your Ideas** Use evidence from the text to support your opinion about whether Charlotte or Uncle Ty is more interesting. Discuss your opinion and evidence with a partner.

_____

_____

Students read text closely to determine what the text says.

**Research Scientific Texts** On a separate sheet of paper or in a new document, take notes on two or three sources about your topic. Record the title, author, and/or URL for the source before you begin taking notes. As you take notes, be sure to use your own words to paraphrase and summarize information from your sources.

**Conventions**

## Perfect Tenses

**DIRECTIONS** Circle the verb in each sentence. On the line next to each sentence, write *PRP* if the verb is in the present perfect tense, *PAP* if the verb is in the past perfect tense, and *FP* if the verb is in the future perfect tense.

1. Dr. Li has studied the planet Venus for the past decade. _____

2. By the end of next year, the institute will have created thousands of new images. _____

3. Corrine and Elliot had watched movies for more than five hours. _____

4. We will have collected enough signatures to submit the petition by next Friday. _____

5. They had finished all of the research for their final paper. _____

 Students write routinely for a range of tasks, purposes, and audiences. Students practice various conventions of standard English.

Name _____

**DIRECTIONS** Write a sentence using each word.

skidded     hesitated     fizzing

_____

_____

_____

_____

**Write in Response to Reading**

How do the illustrations on pages 22–24 help you better understand the story? Use evidence from the text to support your response. Write your response below, on a separate sheet of paper, or in a new document.

_____

_____

_____

_____

_____

Students demonstrate contextual understanding of Benchmark Vocabulary. Students read text closely and use text evidence in their written answers.

## Analyze Images

**DIRECTIONS** Using evidence from the text, answer the following questions about pages 22–24 from *Jess and Layla's Astronomical Assignment*.

1. Look at the illustration on pages 22–23. What details from the story are depicted in the illustration?

   _____

   _____

   _____

2. How does the illustration help you understand the emotions of the scene?

   _____

   _____

3. Look at the illustration on page 24. What details from the story are depicted in the illustration?

   _____

   _____

   _____

4. How does the illustration help you understand Jess and Layla's surprise and confusion?

   _____

   _____

 Students analyze and respond to literary and informational text.

**Research Digital Sources** Find two or three reliable digital sources that will support the main ideas from your outline or plan for writing in Lesson 2. On a separate sheet of paper or in a new document, take one or two pages of notes on these sources.

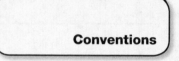

**Conventions**

## Perfect Tenses

**DIRECTIONS** Write a sentence using each verb below in the tense identified.

1. cause (past perfect) _____

   _____

2. work (future perfect) _____

   _____

3. plan (past perfect) _____

   _____

4. listen (present perfect) _____

   _____

5. ask (present perfect) _____

   _____

 Students write routinely for a range of tasks, purposes, and audiences. Students practice various conventions of standard English.

**Unit 3 • Module B • Lesson 4 • 271**

Name _____

**DIRECTIONS** Write a sentence using each word.

afterthought    shrieked    hazily

_____

_____

_____

_____

_____

_____

**Write in Response to Reading**

Write a paragraph that explains how the lesson Dr. Goggles teaches about astronomy affects Layla's choices about what time periods to travel to in the van. Use evidence from the text in your response. Write your response below, on a separate sheet of paper, or in a new document.

_____

_____

_____

_____

_____

_____

Students demonstrate contextual understanding of Benchmark Vocabulary. Students read text closely and use text evidence in their written answers.

**Develop the Topic** Synthesize the information you gathered from sources in Lessons 3 and 4. Review your sources, and determine which information you might quote directly in your informative essay and which information you might include as summaries or paraphrases. Then write or find the proper citations for the information you will use. Finally, draft your essay, developing your topic according to the outline or plan you created in Lesson 2 (or a better structure you have developed) and synthesizing the information from your sources and your own ideas. Write your draft on a separate sheet of paper or in a new document.

**Conventions**

## Use Verb Tense to Convey Sequences

**DIRECTIONS** Fill in each blank with the correct form of the verb in parentheses to create an appropriate sequence of tenses.

1. After William _____ (walk) for nearly ten miles, he finally stopped to rest.

2. Nikki will stay in Maine next summer, but her brother Nick _____ (go) to Florida.

3. Before Sonya _____ (move) to Chicago, she had visited the city twice.

4. Civil rights activists of the 1950s and 1960s knew that segregation

   _____ (be) wrong.

5. Nora realized that she had the wrong workbook after she _____ (answer) all of the questions.

Students write routinely for a range of tasks, purposes, and audiences. Students practice various conventions of standard English.

**Unit 3 • Module B • Lesson 5 • 273**

## Prefix *im-*

**DIRECTIONS** Find the word in the Word Bank that best matches each definition. Write the word on the line.

### Word Bank

| | | | | |
|---|---|---|---|---|
| immense | imbalanced | immemorial | immature | immeasurable |
| immaculate | immobilized | immutable | impalpable | impermanent |
| impermeable | impermissible | imperturbable | implacable | impractical |
| impolite | imponderable | imprecise | improbable | impudent |

_____ **1.** unfair or uneven

_____ **2.** so vast that it cannot be measured

_____ **3.** not allowed according to the rules

_____ **4.** not likely to happen

_____ **5.** prevented from moving

_____ **6.** likely to disappear eventually

_____ **7.** neither courteous nor considerate

_____ **8.** unrealistic, unworkable

_____ **9.** hazy, confusing, and unclear

_____ **10.** not yet full grown

**DIRECTIONS** Read each root and its definition. On the line, write the word from the Word Bank that means the opposite of the root.

**11.** The root *mensus* means "measured." _____

**12.** The root *macula* means "spot" or "blemish." _____

**13.** The root *pudens* means "ashamed." _____

**14.** The root *permeare* means "to pass through." _____

**15.** The root *memoria* means "memory." _____

**16.** The root *mutabilis* means "changeable." _____

**17.** The root *palpabilis* means "that may be felt." _____

**18.** The root *perturbare* means "to disturb." _____

**19.** The root *placabilis* means "easily satisfied." _____

**20.** The root *ponderare* means "consider." _____

 Students apply grade-level phonics and word analysis skills.

Name _____

**DIRECTIONS** Write a sentence using each word.

astonishment    portrait    admirer

_____

_____

_____

**Write in Response to Reading**

Reread page 37. What do you think the word *balderdash* means? What clues from the text helped you determine its meaning? Why do you think Galileo uses the word to describe Pythagoras's model? Write your response below, on a separate sheet of paper, or in a new document.

_____

_____

_____

_____

_____

Students demonstrate contextual understanding of Benchmark Vocabulary. Students read text closely and use text evidence in their written answers.

**Develop and Link Ideas** Develop and link ideas in the essay you drafted in Lesson 5. You can develop your ideas by using and explaining domain-specific words. You can link ideas by using words to show the order in which events occurred, to show cause and effect, to compare and contrast, or to show other relationships between words, phrases, and sentences. First, work with a partner to evaluate each other's work and determine where to add transitions, domain-specific language, and explanations or definitions of domain-specific language. Then write your revised essay on a separate sheet of paper or in a new document.

**Conventions**

## Verb Tense to Convey Sequences

**DIRECTIONS** Write three sentences below that contain a sequence of verbs that includes the present perfect tense. Underline the verb in the present perfect tense in each sentence.

1. _____

   _____

   _____

2. _____

   _____

   _____

3. _____

   _____

   _____

Students write routinely for a range of tasks, purposes, and audiences. Students practice various conventions of standard English.

**DIRECTIONS** Write a sentence using each word.

pompously     sarcastic     bickering

_____

_____

_____

_____

**Write in Response to Reading**

How do the illustrations on pages 39–41 help you better understand the relationship between the different astronomers' ideas? Use evidence from the text in your response. Write your response below, on separate sheet of paper, or in a new document.

_____

_____

_____

_____

_____

_____

Students demonstrate contextual understanding of Benchmark Vocabulary.
Students read text closely and use text evidence in their written answers.

## Use Illustrations

**DIRECTIONS** Using evidence from the text, answer the following questions about pages 39–41 from *Jess and Layla's Astronomical Assignment*.

1. How does this illustration on page 39 help you better understand an important idea or event in the story?

   _____

   _____

   _____

2. How does this illustration on page 40 help you better understand an important idea or event in the story?

   _____

   _____

   _____

3. How does this illustration on page 41 help you better understand an important idea or event in the story?

   _____

   _____

   _____

Students analyze and respond to literary and informational text.

**Incorporate Visuals and Multimedia** Use the steps from the lesson (review, choose, and research) to incorporate visuals and multimedia elements into your informative essay. Link them to your essay by either providing a caption that identifies the illustration or multimedia element or introducing it in your text. On a separate sheet of paper or in a new document, revise your draft to incorporate the visuals or multimedia elements and their captions or introductions in the text.

**Conventions**

## Modal Auxiliaries

**DIRECTIONS** Complete each sentence with an appropriate modal auxiliary verb.

1. Leslie's mother says that she _____ go to the mall with us on Saturday.

2. Winona _____ do her chores before she goes outside to play.

3. Our neighbors _____ become angry if we walk on their lawn.

4. Kyle _____ dance, but he does not want to dance to this song.

5. I know that I _____ get up earlier in the morning, but I am always sleepy.

Students write routinely for a range of tasks, purposes, and audiences. Students practice various conventions of standard English.

Name _____

**DIRECTIONS** Write a sentence using each word.

distraught    detour    hurtled    unison

_____

_____

_____

_____

_____

**Write in Response to Reading**

Reread pages 46–48. Describe how the astronomers respond to one another's ideas as they travel through space. What might a reader learn from their interactions? Use text evidence to support your answer. Write your response below, on a separate sheet of paper, or in a new document.

_____

_____

_____

_____

_____

 Students demonstrate contextual understanding of Benchmark Vocabulary. Students read text closely and use text evidence in their written answers.

**Create a Works Cited List** On a separate sheet of paper or in a new document, create a Works Cited list for your essay. First, identify all of the sources you used in your essay, and determine each source's medium (print, Web site, etc.). Then, use the format provided in the lesson to create a citation reference for each source. Finally, list your sources in alphabetical order.

**Conventions**

## Modal Auxiliaries

**DIRECTIONS** For each modal auxiliary verb, write two sentences using it correctly.

1. can _____

   _____

   _____

   _____

2. could _____

   _____

   _____

   _____

 Students write routinely for a range of tasks, purposes, and audiences. Students practice various conventions of standard English.

Name _____

**DIRECTIONS** Write a sentence using each word.

glittering　　investigated　　souvenir

_____

_____

_____

_____

**Write in Response to Reading**

Choose one of the astronomers from *Jess and Layla's Astronomical Assignment.* Think about his dialogue and behavior. Describe his personality and some ways it was or wasn't what you expected for a historical scientist. Use text evidence to support your answer. Write your response below, on a separate sheet of paper, or in a new document.

_____

_____

_____

_____

_____

Students demonstrate contextual understanding of Benchmark Vocabulary. Students read text closely and use text evidence in their written answers.

**Develop a Conclusion**  On a separate sheet of paper or in a new document, write a concluding paragraph for your research paper. Develop a transition sentence to introduce the conclusion, identify and briefly summarize the main points of the essay, and offer additional insight based on what you learned while drafting your research paper.

**Conventions**

## Use Consistent Verb Tenses

**DIRECTIONS**  Underline both verbs in each sentence or sentence pair. Change the second verb to make the tense consistent, and write the new verb on the line.

1. Uranus's moon Miranda <u>features</u> huge canyons, ropelike markings, and deep grooves. Ridges also <u>marked</u> its surfaces. _____

2. Pythagoras also <u>studied</u> mathematics and <u>proves</u> the Pythagorean theorem. _____

3. The astronomer Tycho Brahe <u>lost</u> his nose in a sword fight! He <u>makes</u> a new nose out of copper. _____

4. Some people <u>call</u> Venus the sister planet to Earth because it <u>was</u> similar in size. _____

5. Halley's Comet <u>will return</u> in 2061 and then <u>is</u> visible again 75 years later. _____

Students write routinely for a range of tasks, purposes, and audiences. Students practice various conventions of standard English.

Name _____

**DIRECTIONS** Write a sentence using each word.

gazed    muttering    filed    sculptures

_____

_____

_____

_____

_____

**Write in Response to Reading**

Look at the time line on page 64. Write the sequence of events from the story in the order they would appear on the time line. Why do you think the author chose to describe the events as they are experienced by Jess and Layla, rather than in the order they occurred in history? Write your response below, on a separate sheet of paper, or in a new document.

_____

_____

_____

_____

_____

 Students demonstrate contextual understanding of Benchmark Vocabulary. Students read text closely and use text evidence in their written answers.

**Story Structure**

**DIRECTIONS** Using evidence from the text, answer the following questions about *Jess and Layla's Astronomical Assignment.*

1. In what order did Jess and Layla meet the astronomers? Why do you think this order was chosen?

   _____

   _____

   _____

   _____

2. Tycho Brahe was an astronomer who believed the Sun revolved around the Earth and the other planets revolved around the Sun. If he were in this story, when do you think Jess and Layla would have picked him up?

   _____

   _____

   _____

   _____

3. On page 62, Jade Jefferson says, "Copernicus ate my homework." What does she mean?

   _____

   _____

   _____

4. Why do you think this detail is included?

   _____

   _____

   _____

Students analyze and respond to literary and informational text.

**Research a Current Topic** On separate sheets of paper or in a new document, draft one to two pages of notes about a recent discovery related to the solar system. List the source information for each article you review, using the formats for citation that you learned in Lesson 8 of this unit. Then briefly summarize the main ideas of each article, and explain what relevant information the article offers about your topic.

## Consistency in Verb Tense

**DIRECTIONS** Underline all the verbs. Write *C* if the verb tenses are consistent and *I* if they are inconsistent. If you write *I*, change the verbs in the second sentence to make the tenses consistent and correct.

1. Comets <u>orbit</u> the sun, but they <u>are</u> quite unlike planets. A comet <u>changed</u> when it

   <u>swept</u> past the sun. _____

2. Mercury <u>is</u> the fastest planet. It <u>orbits</u> the sun once every 116 days. _____

   _____

3. Mars <u>has</u> two moons, Phobos and Deimos. They <u>were</u> strangely shaped, so

   scientists think they <u>will be</u> actually captured asteroids. _____

4. Neil Armstrong and Buzz Aldrin <u>were</u> the first people on the moon. The third
   member of the team, Michael Collins, <u>will stay</u> behind in the command module.

   _____

5. It <u>will probably be</u> a couple decades before a manned ship <u>will visit</u> Mars.

   The trip <u>took</u> several weeks. _____

Students write routinely for a range of tasks, purposes, and audiences. Students practice various conventions of standard English.

Name _____

## Acronyms

**DIRECTIONS** Draw a line to match each acronym on the left with its source on the right.

1. AWOL      Organization of Petroleum Exporting Countries

2. SCUBA      read-only memory

3. radar      radio detecting and ranging

4. NATO      unknown subject

5. sonar      absent without leave

6. OPEC      self-contained underwater breathing apparatus

7. SCOTUS      North Atlantic Treaty Organization

8. UNSUB      Supreme Court of the United States

9. SARS      sound navigation and ranging

10. ROM      severe acute respiratory syndrome

 Students apply grade-level phonics and word analysis skills.

**DIRECTIONS** Write a sentence using each word.

unpredictable    accumulated    hypothesis    theory    revolutionary

_____

_____

_____

_____

_____

_____

_____

**Write in Response to Reading**

Agree or disagree with the following statement: Visual elements in informative texts are most effective when combined with other visual elements. Write a paragraph using reasons, facts, and details from the text to support your point of view. Write your response below, on a separate sheet of paper, or in a new document.

_____

_____

_____

_____

_____

_____

 Students demonstrate contextual understanding of Benchmark Vocabulary. Students read text closely and use text evidence in their written answers.

**Evaluate Sources**  Evaluate your sources from Lesson 10, and put aside those that are not relevant, credible, current, or accurate. If there are any gaps in information, further research may be necessary to fully address all aspects of the topic. After reviewing and organizing your notes, write one page synthesizing all your sources on a separate sheet of paper or in a new document. On another sheet of paper or another page in your document, write a correctly formatted Works Cited page listing all the print and digital sources you used in your one-page report.

**Conventions**

## Adjectives

**DIRECTIONS**  Circle the adjective in each sentence below. Then underline the noun it modifies. (Ignore all articles.)

1. The twin telescopes are located on the summit of Mauna Kea in Hawaii.

2. Stonehenge in England was used as an astronomical calendar.

3. The Jovian planets are also called gas giants.

4. Scientist believe the dinosaurs were killed when a large asteroid struck the Earth.

5. Some describe Pluto as a trans-Neptunian object.

Students write routinely for a range of tasks, purposes, and audiences. Students practice various conventions of standard English.

**Benchmark Vocabulary**

**DIRECTIONS** Write a sentence using each word.

recognized          churning

_____

_____

_____

**Write in Response to Reading**

Read pages 16–21. Write an explanatory paragraph, including text evidence, about the ways that astronomers classify stars. Write your paragraph below, on a separate sheet of paper, or in a new document.

_____

_____

_____

_____

_____

Students demonstrate contextual understanding of Benchmark Vocabulary. Students read text closely and use text evidence in their written answers.

## Domain-Specific Vocabulary

**DIRECTIONS** Using evidence from the text, answer the following questions about pages 18–19 from *Our Mysterious Universe*.

1. What is a neutron star?

   When the massive star finally collapses its core forms a very dense neutron star.

2. What is a supernova?

   When a neutrons stars outer layer explodes into space it produces a super nova.

3. What is a black hole?

   A black hole is a dense object that not even light can escape its gravity.

4. Explain how neutron stars, supernovas, and black holes are related.

Students analyze and respond to literary and informational text.

**Plan an Informative Journal Article**  Plan an informative journal article by first reviewing the sources you used in Lesson 10 and the page you wrote in Lesson 11. Next, consider how to use the journal article format to present your research about a recent important discovery related to space exploration. Then clearly state the topic you will write about and indicate the article's focus. Finally, on separate sheets of paper or in a new document, use a graphic organizer to show how you will group information in your journal article and make notes about visual elements that would enhance your article. Be sure to consider your purpose (to inform) and your audience (other students).

**Conventions**

## Adverbs

**DIRECTIONS**  Underline the adverbs in the sentences below. Then draw two lines under the word or words each adverb modifies.

1. Energy built up in the sun's atmosphere suddenly releases.

2. The solar heat quickly turns some of the comet's snow to a gas.

3. The Very Large Array is an observatory with a very boring name.

4. Supernovas shine brightly before fading away.

5. Traveling at that speed is physically impossible.

Students write routinely for a range of tasks, purposes, and audiences. Students practice various conventions of standard English.

**DIRECTIONS** Write a sentence using each word.

expanding     interacted

_____

_____

_____

_____

**Write in Response to Reading**

What piece of technology is more important: the Hubble Space Telescope or the Arecibo dish? Use details from the text to write a paragraph supporting your opinion. Write your response below, on a separate sheet of paper, or in a new document.

_____

_____

_____

_____

_____

_____

Students demonstrate contextual understanding of Benchmark Vocabulary. Students read text closely and use text evidence in their written answers.

## Moving to Mars?

I was thinking last week about what it would be like if I moved to another planet. I see some advantages right away, of course. First, I might get my name into the history books as the First Resident in Space, which would be totally awesome. Second, it would be a great opportunity to get away from the bully down the street. And third, a planet like Mars has so little gravity that people can jump about three times higher there than they can on Earth. With a vertical leap like that, I'd be virtually unstoppable on the basketball court.

But I recognize downsides to the idea, too. For one thing, moving is a humongous hassle. Even if you just move across the state, you need to pack, say goodbye to neighbors, and take care of a lot of other stuff. Now imagine how much worse that would be if you were moving across the solar system. If you forget to pack even one thing, you might never see it again. And as for connecting with family and friends, I don't think you can rely on webcams on Mercury.

Then there's the little problem of always having to wear a space suit. Did you know that Earth is the only planet with enough oxygen to keep us alive? Temperatures are another big issue. It gets up to 460°C (860°F) on Venus—hot enough to fry not just an egg but also a person. As for Saturn, even the most powerful furnaces in the universe aren't going to keep you warm when it's around –178°C (–288°F) outdoors. I guess you'd probably live in a big dome so you could move around some, but not getting to go outside at all—that's harsh.

Oh, and a lot of these planets are—well, let's just say that they're not like Earth. For instance, Jupiter consists mostly of gases like hydrogen and helium, so there isn't exactly anywhere to stand, let alone to play basketball. Venus has almost zero water, so can you imagine the cost of trying to ship some in from Earth? And the gusts on Neptune are almost ten times stronger than the winds we get here—good for extreme kite-flying, I guess, but not for much else.

So all in all, I plan on staying here on Earth if folks begin settling the other planets. Definitely. It's the only decision that makes any sense.

 Students read text closely to determine what the text says.

**Gather Evidence** Underline the three advantages that the writer gives as reasons for moving to another planet.

**Gather Evidence: Extend Your Ideas** Which of the three underlined advantages includes factual evidence?

_____

_____

**Ask Questions** What two questions would you ask about Mars, Mercury, Venus, Saturn, Jupiter, or Neptune?

_____

_____

**Ask Questions: Extend Your Ideas** Look at the two questions you wrote. List one print and one online source you could use to find the answers to your questions.

_____

**Make Your Case** The writer mentions several obstacles in his case for space settlement. Which is the most effective?

_____

_____

**Make Your Case: Extend Your Ideas** Even though there are many obstacles to living on another planet, do you think you would want to settle elsewhere in the solar system someday? Discuss your opinion with a partner.

_____

 Students read text closely to determine what the text says.

**Draft an Informative Journal Article** Begin drafting your informative journal article based on your graphic organizer from Lesson 12. First, review your notes on sources and select facts, concrete details, and examples. Next, choose interesting images to accompany the facts and details in your journal article. Then, on separate sheets of paper or in a new document, write a rough draft of your journal article. Include an introduction, body paragraphs that present factual information, and a conclusion that summarizes the topic and makes a suggestion for further research. Be sure to properly cite all sources for both written information and images. If possible, also create layouts showing what information and visual elements you will include in a presentation.

**Conventions**

## Linking Verbs and Subject Complements

**DIRECTIONS** In each sentence, circle the subject of the sentence and underline its subject complement.

1. Edwin Hubble was a famous astronomer who measured the red shift.

2. The astronomer who measured the red shift was he.

3. The first person to go to outer space was Yuri Gagarin.

4. Perhaps the first human on Mars will be you!

5. Saturn's largest moon is Titan.

 Students write routinely for a range of tasks, purposes, and audiences. Students practice various conventions of standard English.

**DIRECTIONS**  Write a sentence using each word.

hypothesis    theory    astronomy

_____

_____

_____

_____

**Write in Response to Reading**

How might Jess and Layla's adventure have changed if they met Edwin Hubble?
What would he say to Jess and Layla? What would he say to the other astronomers?
Where or when would he want to go in the van? Use evidence from the texts to support
your answers. Write your response below, on a separate sheet of paper, or in a new
document.

_____

_____

_____

_____

_____

_____

Students demonstrate contextual understanding of
Benchmark Vocabulary. Students read text closely
and use text evidence in their written answers.

**Revise or Rewrite an Informative Journal Article** Peer review a partner's informative journal article, recording your comments on a separate sheet of paper or a new document. Evaluate the organization of your partner's article. Identify any vague language in your partner's article, and suggest precise or domain-specific language to use instead. Suggest where to include visuals in your partner's article. Then, on a separate sheet of paper or in a new document, revise and edit your own journal article based on your peer's feedback.

**Conventions**

## Linking Verbs and Subject Complements

**DIRECTIONS** In each sentence, circle the subject of the sentence and underline its subject complement.

1. Quasars seemed quite small.

2. Neptune is one of the Jovian planets.

3. Laika the dog became the first animal to orbit Earth.

4. Scientists think a planet called Theia crashed into Earth a long time ago, and the

   debris became the moon.

5. In many science fiction stories, black holes are doorways to other times and

   places because they are so mysterious.

 Students write routinely for a range of tasks, purposes, and audiences. Students practice various conventions of standard English.

Name _____

**DIRECTIONS**  Write a sentence using each word.

inescapable    intense    boundary    frenzy

_____

_____

_____

_____

_____

**Write in Response to Reading**

Which examples of imagery best describe black holes? Use text evidence to support your opinion. Write your response below, on a separate sheet of paper, or in a new document.

_____

_____

_____

_____

_____

Students demonstrate contextual understanding of Benchmark Vocabulary. Students read text closely and use text evidence in their written answers.

Name _____

## Imagery and Repetition

**DIRECTIONS** Using evidence from the text, answer the following questions about pages 30–35 of *A Black Hole is NOT a Hole.*

1. What phrase is repeated on the first page of the selection?

   _____

2. Why is this phrase important?

   _____

   _____

3. What is the effect of this repetition?

   _____

   _____

   _____

4. Look at page 35. What phrase on this page is similar to the repeated phrase above?

   _____

5. Remember that a simile compares two different things using the words *like* or *as*. What does the simile on page 35 compare?

   _____

   _____

6. How does this image help you visualize black holes?

   _____

   _____

 Students analyze and respond to literary and informational text.

**Edit and Proofread an Informative Journal Article** Review the edited and proofread draft of your informative journal article. Then ask your partner any questions you have about his or her edits. Finally, on separate sheets of paper or in a new document, write or type an updated version of your journal article, incorporating your partner's changes.

Conventions

### Degrees of Comparison

**DIRECTIONS** In each sentence, underline the adjective or adverb that shows a degree of comparison. After each sentence, write *CD* if it is comparative or *SD* if it is superlative.

1. Jupiter is the largest planet in our solar system. _____ .

2. The large meteorite burned brighter than the comet that passed close to Earth. _____

3. A black hole's pull is the strongest pull in the entire universe. _____

4. Globular clusters are bigger and brighter than open clusters. _____

5. Aristotle was not only an astronomer but was also a researcher of biology and physics and is considered one of the greatest philosophers in the world. _____

Students write routinely for a range of tasks, purposes, and audiences. Students practice various conventions of standard English.

## Greek and Latin Roots

**DIRECTIONS** Write the word from the Word Bank that best summarizes each group. Use a dictionary for help if you wish.

### Word Bank

| journalism | manuscript | phobia | ecology | prescription |
|---|---|---|---|---|
| heroism | disrupt | telescope | grammar | spectacle |
| pedometer | patriot | pyrotechnic | mathematics | vocalist |

1. soprano, alto, bass, baritone _____

2. fear, panic, anxiety _____

3. living things, the environment, interactions _____

4. love of country, loyalty to the flag _____

5. public show, elaborate performance _____

6. upset, break apart, force to change _____

7. writing, reporting, news _____

8. rough draft, unpublished book _____

9. distance, watch, start, space _____

10. courage, bravery, fortitude _____

11. letters, sentences, literature _____

12. brilliant, gleaming, like fireworks _____

13. addition, subtraction, multiplication, division _____

14. walk, steps, measure _____

15. instructions, orders, formula _____

 Students apply grade-level phonics and word analysis skills.

Name _____

**DIRECTIONS** Write a sentence using each word.

colossal     imploded     relatively     intermediate     probe     symmetric

_____

_____

_____

_____

_____

_____

_____

**Write in Response to Reading**

Choose a domain-specific vocabulary word from the text, and write a paragraph summarizing how the author uses it to explain a concept. Write your response below, on a separate sheet of paper, or in a new document.

_____

_____

_____

_____

_____

Students demonstrate contextual understanding of Benchmark Vocabulary. Students read text closely and use text evidence in their written answers.

Name _____

**Publish and Present an Informative Journal Article** On separate sheets of paper or in a new document, make a clean copy of the latest draft of your informative journal article. Highlight main ideas and key details that you want to include in a presentation, and take notes on the information. Consider how to introduce the topic to engage the audience, and choose or create relevant visuals to add to your presentation. If possible, use publishing software to make a presentation. Finally, deliver an oral presentation based on your article.

**Conventions**

## Degrees of Comparison

**DIRECTIONS** Read the sentences and look at the underlined adjective or adverb. Determine what degree of comparison it is and add it to the chart. Then fill in the other degrees of comparison.

1. Being sucked into a black hole would be downright <u>scary.</u>

2. The <u>most intriguing</u> aspect of a black hole is how it gets started.

3. A supermassive black hole is much <u>more exciting</u> than a regular black hole.

| Question | Positive Degree | Comparative Degree | Superlative Degree |
|----------|-----------------|--------------------|--------------------|
| 1 | | | |
| 2 | | | |
| 3 | | | |

Students write routinely for a range of tasks, purposes, and audiences. Students practice various conventions of standard English.

Name _____

**DIRECTIONS** Write a sentence using each word.

inspiration     intense

_____

_____

_____

_____

**Write in Response to Reading**

How do these texts explain scientific concepts in a way that is memorable and understandable? Which text do you think is more effective and why? Write your response below, on a separate sheet of paper, or in a new document.

_____

_____

_____

_____

_____

Students demonstrate contextual understanding of Benchmark Vocabulary. Students read text closely and use text evidence in their written answers.

# Lesson 17

Name _____

**Compare and Contrast Texts** Begin by reviewing the texts and then create an outline based on the similarities and differences listed in your T-chart or Venn diagram. Choose the best organization for your essay and be sure to include concrete and relevant details from each text.

## Irregular Comparisons

**DIRECTIONS** Circle the word in parentheses that correctly completes the sentence.

1. Uranus is (farest/farther) from the Sun than Mercury is.

2. We can all feel (betterest/good) about the results of the latest astronomy experiment.

3. The (best/goodest) black hole images taken with the telescope camera will be published in a book.

4. The explosion of the space shuttle was one of the (worsest/worst) disasters in the history of spaceflight.

5. I don't know astronomy very (well/weller); I thought a pulsar was a science fiction device.

 Students write routinely for a range of tasks, purposes, and audiences. Students practice various conventions of standard English.

Name _____

**DIRECTIONS** Write a sentence using each word.

universe     revolutionary     probe

_____

_____

_____

_____

**Write in Response to Reading**

Write a short explanatory paragraph about our solar system and where it fits into the universe. Write your response below, on a separate sheet of paper, or in a new document.

_____

_____

_____

_____

_____

_____

Students demonstrate contextual understanding of Benchmark Vocabulary. Students read text closely and use text evidence in their written answers.

Name _____

## Compare and Contrast Genres

**DIRECTIONS** Using evidence from the texts, answer the following questions about *Jess and Layla's Astronomical Assignment, Our Mysterious Universe,* and *A Black Hole is NOT a Hole.*

1. What does each text have to say about stars?

_____

_____

_____

_____

_____

2. What is the genre of each text?

_____

_____

_____

3. Which text do you think is most effective in expressing scientific concepts? Explain your answer.

_____

_____

_____

 Students analyze and respond to literary and informational text.

**Lesson 18**

Name _____

**Develop a Compare-Contrast Essay**  On separate sheets of paper or in a new document, develop a compare-contrast essay. First, organize your draft using your outline from Lesson 17. Include well-organized text evidence (facts, details, examples, and quotes) from the texts. Use transitions to link ideas within paragraphs and between paragraphs, and include a strong conclusion that highlights the significance of the similarities or differences across texts.

**Conventions**

## Avoiding Double Comparisons

**DIRECTIONS**  Write *C* if the underlined comparisons are correct and *I* if they are incorrect. If you write *I*, write the correct form of the comparison.

1. Neptune is <u>most farthest</u> from the sun than any other planet in the solar system.

   _____

2. I think the <u>best</u> view of Venus is at dusk. _____

3. The issue of "space junk" is becoming <u>more worse</u> every year.

   _____

4. If our sun were <u>more bigger,</u> it would eventually go supernova.

   _____

5. Finding extraterrestrial life could be the <u>most importantest</u> scientific discovery in

   history. _____

Students write routinely for a range of tasks, purposes, and audiences. Students practice various conventions of standard English.

Name _____

## Complex Spelling Patterns

**DIRECTIONS** Use the ending -*ous*, -*eous*, or -*ious* to change the underlined noun in each sentence to an adjective. On the line, write a new sentence with the new adjective. The new sentence may, but does not have to, say the same thing as the original sentence.

1. Drake experienced an attack of <u>nerves</u>.

   _____

2. Marla's behavior toward the queen was a model of <u>courtesy</u>.

   _____

3. The virus is quite likely to cause an <u>infection</u>.

   _____

4. That question always gets a <u>variety</u> of answers.

   _____

5. Leon's new bedroom has an incredible amount of <u>space</u>.

   _____

6. Have you ever known a person who is full of <u>ambition</u>?

   _____

7. Randy was full of <u>fury</u> when he got the letter with his score.

   _____

8. Please exercise <u>caution</u> when you climb down the ladder.

   _____

9. Neptune, Jupiter, Saturn, and Uranus are made mostly of <u>gas</u>.

   _____

10. The baby birds whose mother flew away cause me to feel <u>pity</u>.

    _____

 Students apply grade-level phonics and word analysis skills.

Name _____

**DIRECTIONS** Write a sentence using each word.

route     legendary     trade     secretive

_____

_____

_____

_____

_____

_____

**Write in Response to Reading**

Write two paragraphs stating and supporting your opinion as to how well the author organizes information about Marco Polo's life. If you were the author, would you have organized the information differently? Write your response below, on a separate sheet of paper, or in a new document.

_____

_____

_____

_____

_____

Students demonstrate contextual understanding of Benchmark Vocabulary. Students read text closely and use text evidence in their written answers.

**Analyze Author's Viewpoint** On a separate sheet of paper or in a new document, write three or four paragraphs explaining how the author uses his purpose and viewpoint to shape the information on pages 4–7 of *Explorers: Triumphs and Troubles.* Use specific examples from the text to support your ideas.

**Conventions**

## Verbals: Gerunds

**DIRECTIONS** Complete the sentences by using the present participle form (the gerund) of the verbs in parentheses.

1. _____ (travel) to the South Pole was dangerous.

2. The writer whom Marco Polo met in prison aided history by _____ (document) the explorer's journey.

3. _____ (find) a new route to Asia was Christopher Columbus's goal.

4. Some explorers concentrated on _____ (race) to be the first to reach a location.

5. Other explorers focused on _____ (look) for silver and gold.

Students write routinely for a range of tasks, purposes, and audiences. Students practice various conventions of standard English.

## Morphemes

**DIRECTIONS** Use the given base word and one or more word parts from the Morpheme Bank to create a new word that matches each definition. Write the new word on the line.

### Morpheme Bank

| im- | bi- | un- | pro- | -ed |
|-----|-----|-----|------|-----|
| -ly | -ize | -ous | -tion | -able |

1. comfort: not able to experience comfort _____

2. annual: two times a year _____

3. introduce: the act of introducing _____

4. maximum: make the largest it can be _____

5. poison: causing illness or death _____

6. expect: with a surprising effect _____

7. theory: what people who develop theories do _____

8. motion: advancement to the next level _____

9. polite: with a lack of politeness _____

10. deny: must be acknowledged _____

**DIRECTIONS** Identify the morphemes in each word. On the line, show the morphemes by writing the letters that represent each one, leaving a space between each set. For example: **im person al.**

_____ **11.** forgetful

_____ **12.** remarkable

_____ **13.** semiconductor

_____ **14.** resettlement

_____ **15.** preapproval

Students apply grade-level phonics and word analysis skills.

Name _____

**DIRECTIONS** Write a sentence using each word.

banned    scorched    campaign    territory

_____

_____

_____

_____

**Write in Response to Reading**

Read pages 8–11. Write an explanatory paragraph about the "official" and "unofficial" reasons Francis Younghusband visited Tibet. What were his suspicions about the country? Write your response below, on a separate sheet of paper, or in a new document.

_____

_____

_____

_____

_____

 Students demonstrate contextual understanding of Benchmark Vocabulary. Students read text closely and use text evidence in their written answers.

Name _____

## Historical Context

**DIRECTIONS** Using evidence from the text, answer the following questions about pages 8–11 from *Explorers: Triumphs and Troubles*.

1. Look at the map on page 8. How does it help the reader understand Younghusband's reasons for leading an expedition to Tibet?

   _____

   _____

2. Why did the Tibetans block the road to Lhasa?

   _____

   _____

3. Why did the British choose not to turn back when they saw the road was blocked?

   _____

   _____

   _____

4. What effect did the Tibetan's "scorched earth" campaign have? Explain.

   _____

   _____

   _____

5. What did the British make the Tibetans do in order for the British to stop occupying part of their territory?

   _____

   _____

 Students analyze and respond to literary and informational text.

**Analyze Visual Elements** Write three paragraphs analyzing how the author uses visuals. First, find one or two images in the sections you have read so far. Second, briefly state the author's viewpoint or purpose. Last, explain how each image you chose either helps the author achieve his purpose or adds support in general. Some images may do both. Write your paragraphs on a separate sheet of paper or in a new document.

**Conventions**

## Verbals: Participles

**DIRECTIONS** Underline the participle used as an adjective in each sentence.

1. The advancing British soldiers attacked the Tibetans.

2. The infuriated Tibetans tried to hold off the British.

3. The British soldiers' sparkling weapons flashed in the sun.

4. The Tibetans tried the "scorched earth" campaign.

5. The British forced the defeated Tibetans to sign an agreement.

Students write routinely for a range of tasks, purposes, and audiences. Students practice various conventions of standard English.

Name _____

**DIRECTIONS** Write a sentence using each word.

     temples    fortune    technically    rival    tactic    ruthless

_____

_____

_____

_____

_____

_____

_____

**Write in Response to Reading**

Read pages 12–15. Write a paragraph that discusses the author's use of adjectives and adverbs in the text. How do the adjectives and adverbs add to the reader's understanding of the text? Write your response below, on a separate sheet of paper, or in a new document.

_____

_____

_____

_____

_____

_____

Students demonstrate contextual understanding of Benchmark Vocabulary. Students read text closely and use text evidence in their written answers.

## A Man of Persistence

Explorer Sir Ernest Shackleton might be the most persistent man who ever lived. On December 5, 1914, he and twenty-seven men set out on a ship called *Endurance*. They hoped to reach the Antarctic continent and become the first people to cross the land on foot.

Despite the predictions of a terrible winter, *Endurance* left South Georgia Island, a remote island in the southern Atlantic Ocean. It headed for Vahsel Bay on Antarctica. Just two days later, the vessel ran into pack ice. For the next six weeks, the ship wove through ice floes.

On January 18, 1915, one day short of landing, the ship hit another thick pack ice. By the next morning, ice had enclosed the ship. Shackleton soon realized the ship was securely stuck in the ice and would remain stuck through many long winter months. During this time, Shackleton had his crew stick to their routines and exercise the sled dogs they had brought with them.

Ten months later, the crew still remained on board. In October 1915, pressure from the ice began to damage the ship, and it began slowly sinking. Shackleton and his crew abandoned the ship and made camp on the surrounding ice. On November 21, 1915, *Endurance* sank completely.

The crew camped on the ice for several months, and in April 1916, the ice floe broke in half, causing the crew to flee in lifeboats. Days later, they landed on Elephant Island, about 350 miles from where the *Endurance* sank.

Shackleton knew he had to take a drastic step if they were ever to be rescued. Elephant Island was too remote for a rescue attempt. So a group of six men set off in a lifeboat for South Georgia Island, where their journey had begun.

The lifeboat landed on the west side of South Georgia Island in May 1916. The whaling stations—the only source of rescue—were on the east side. Shackleton and two others left on foot to travel the twenty-two miles to the nearest stations.

Within thirty-six hours, the men had made it to a whaling station and began planning the crew's rescue. Finally, on August 30, 1916, the crew was rescued from Elephant Island. After almost two years, the ordeal was over, and not one crew member had died. It was an amazing expedition with a happy ending because of one man's persistence to bring everyone home.

Students read text closely to determine what the text says.

**Gather Evidence**  Underline events that highlight Shackleton's persistence.

**Gather Evidence: Extend Your Ideas**  Add brackets around the events that caused Shackleton to draw on his personal resolve and determination.

**Ask Questions**  Write two questions you would ask a crew member about Shackleton's leadership skills.

` _____

_____

**Ask Questions: Extend Your Ideas**  Write an additional question about Shackleton's leadership skills that is answered in the text. Circle the answer in the text.

_____

_____

**Make Your Case**  How important was Shackleton's persistence to himself and the crew of the *Endurance*?

_____

_____

**Make Your Case: Extend Your Ideas**  Use evidence from the text to support your opinion about which act of Shackleton's was the bravest. Discuss your results with a partner.

_____

_____

 Students read text closely to determine what the text says.

**Analyze Author's Style** Select a passage from the sections of *Explorers: Triumphs and Trouble*s the class has read so far. The passage should include at least one full paragraph. Make sure you select a passage in which you think the author's style reinforces his viewpoint or his purpose. After you select a passage, study sentence length and variety. You might want to use an organizer to list interesting or unusual words and phrases, idioms and other examples of familiar language, and descriptive details or striking images. Highlight figurative language. Then, on a separate sheet of paper or in a new document, write three or more paragraphs analyzing the author's style and explaining how it affects your response to the author's viewpoint. Use text evidence to support your points.

**Conventions**

## Verbals: Infinitives

**DIRECTIONS** Underline the infinitives in each sentence from pages 12–13 of *Explorers: Triumphs and Troubles.*

1. They went to find riches, and they weren't afraid to fight for them.

2. Their next step was to take over the mainland of Mexico.

3. The Aztec temples were said to be full of gold.

4. On hearing this, Cortés decided to head for Tenochtitlán, the Aztec capital city, to find his fortune.

5. However, the Tlaxcalan leaders then decided to join the Spanish conquistadors.

 Students write routinely for a range of tasks, purposes, and audiences. Students practice various conventions of standard English.

**DIRECTIONS** Write a sentence using each word.

limitless    fierce    mythical    brilliant    catastrophe

_____

_____

_____

_____

_____

_____

_____

**Write in Response to Reading**

Read pages 16–19. Using details from the text, write an informative paragraph that explains what Orellana's actions in the New World reveal about him. Write your response below, on a separate sheet of paper, or in a new document.

_____

_____

_____

_____

_____

_____

Students demonstrate contextual understanding of Benchmark Vocabulary. Students read text closely and use text evidence in their written answers.

**Develop an Opinion Statement and Introduction** Write an introduction for an opinion essay that responds to the following question about explorers' motivations: Did explorers desire personal gain, or were they intent on advancing people's knowledge of the world? Write your introduction on a separate sheet of paper or in a new document.

**Conventions**

## Prepositions

**DIRECTIONS** Circle the prepositions in each sentence from pages 16–19 of *Explorers: Triumphs and Troubles.*

1. He was said to be a local ruler with almost limitless supplies of gold, and the conquistadors wanted to get their hands on it!

2. At first, things did not go well for Orellana and his men—they got so hungry searching for food that they ate the boiled soles of their shoes!

3. Orellana claimed that his men refused to return to their companions, and the river's powerful flow made it impossible anyway.

4. A fierce band of what they thought were women then attacked the explorers.

5. Orellana was a ruthless adventurer, prepared to cheat and kill for wealth.

 Students write routinely for a range of tasks, purposes, and audiences. Students practice various conventions of standard English.

Name _____

**DIRECTIONS** Write a sentence using each word.

heroic     Aboriginal     indigenous

_____

_____

_____

_____

**Write in Response to Reading**

What do you think is the author's point of view about Scott's journey to the South Pole? Use evidence from the text to support your answer. Write your response below, on a separate sheet of paper, or in a new document.

_____

_____

_____

_____

_____

_____

Students demonstrate contextual understanding of Benchmark Vocabulary. Students read text closely and use text evidence in their written answers.

## Determine Viewpoint

**DIRECTIONS**  Using evidence from the text, answer the following questions about pages 20–25 from *Explorers: Triumphs and Troubles*.

1. On page 20, the author writes that Scott "prepared carefully for the journey." Why do you think the author provides this detail?

   _____

   _____

   _____

2. Does the author consider Scott's expedition a success because his team reached the South Pole, or does the author consider the expedition a failure because none of the team's members made it back alive?

   _____

   _____

   _____

3. What is the author's viewpoint about the conflict he describes in the first paragraph on page 24? How do you know?

   _____

   _____

   _____

4. How is this viewpoint supported by the author's use of details on pages 24–25?

   _____

   _____

   _____

   _____

Students analyze and respond to literary and informational text.

**Gather Evidence** On a separate sheet of paper or in a new document, write complete sentences for each reason in your graphic organizer, using details that support your viewpoint.

**Conventions**

## Prepositional Phrases

**DIRECTIONS** Circle the prepositions in each sentence from pages 20–25 of *Explorers: Triumphs and Troubles*. Then underline the prepositional phrases.

1. In 1911, no explorer had ever reached the South Pole.

2. Scott prepared carefully for the journey.

3. Their journey from Britain to Australia had taken 250 days, and they had endured storms, shortages of food and water, and even a mutiny.

4. They thought this allowed them to claim the territory for Britain.

5. By 1790, many Eora were frustrated by the new arrivals.

 Students write routinely for a range of tasks, purposes, and audiences. Students practice various conventions of standard English.

**Prefixes** *over-, in-*

**DIRECTIONS** Read the paragraph. Identify each word that contains either the prefix *over-* or the prefix *in-*. Write those words to the left of the numbers below, and write a definition for the word on the right. Feel free to consult a dictionary for help.

The insufferable heat beat down on the overheated engine. Big birds circled overhead. Sally and Patrick rested in the inadequate shade of a cactus. Soon, the noon sun would overtake the shadow. Sally's inefficient phone searched for a signal; the emergency number she tried had been inactivated. Patrick was incapable of overcoming his regret. He had overlooked the jugs of water when they left.

_____ 1. _____

_____ 2. _____

_____ 3. _____

_____ 4. _____

_____ 5. _____

_____ 6. _____

_____ 7. _____

_____ 8. _____

_____ 9. _____

_____ 10. _____

**DIRECTIONS** Add the prefix *over-* or the prefix *in-* to each base word in parentheses. Then use the word to complete the sentence. You will have to adjust the ending of the word to make it fit in the sentence. Feel free to consult a dictionary or thesaurus for help.

11. Sally's positive attitude was (destroy), however. _____

12. At first, the approaching truck was (audio). _____

13. Very quickly, though, its arrival was (escape)! _____

14. (Joy), Sally yanked Patrick to his feet. _____

15. They jumped and yelled with (power) feelings of relief. _____

Students apply grade-level phonics and word analysis skills.

Name _____

**DIRECTIONS** Write a sentence using each word.

venomous    exhausted    ambition    contempt    decimated

_____

_____

_____

_____

_____

_____

_____

**Write in Response to Reading**

Use time-order words such as *first, next,* and *last* to describe the events on pages 26–29 in *Explorers: Triumphs and Troubles* in order. Write your response below, on a separate sheet of paper, or in a new document.

_____

_____

_____

_____

_____

_____

Students demonstrate contextual understanding of Benchmark Vocabulary. Students read text closely and use text evidence in their written answers.

**Organize Reasons and Evidence** Order the evidence you gathered in the previous lesson in a logical way that makes sense to you (for instance, order of importance, time order, or cause/effect), and show the order in an outline. Write your point of view about explorers' motivations at the top, and support it with at least three different pieces of evidence. Write your opinion and outline on a separate sheet of paper or in a new document.

**Conventions**

## Prepositional Phrases and Compound Objects

**DIRECTIONS** On the lines below, write five sentences that include prepositional phrases with compound objects.

1. _____
   _____

2. _____
   _____

3. _____
   _____

4. _____
   _____

5. _____
   _____

Students write routinely for a range of tasks, purposes, and audiences. Students practice various conventions of standard English.

**DIRECTIONS** Write a sentence using each word.

fortune    limitless    ambition    traditional    property

_____

_____

_____

_____

_____

_____

_____

**Write in Response to Reading**

Read pages 26–29 of *Explorers: Triumphs and Troubles*. What factors led to Burke's failure to reach the north coast of Australia, his death, and the deaths of some of his men? Support your opinion with text evidence. Write your response below, on a separate sheet of paper, or in a new document.

_____

_____

_____

_____

_____

Students demonstrate contextual understanding of Benchmark Vocabulary. Students read text closely and use text evidence in their written answers.

Name _____

**Strengthen Reasons and Evidence**  Draft, peer review, and revise your essay, using your outline from the previous lesson to guide you. Remember that when you review your partner's feedback and begin the revision process, you should look back over each chapter of the text in search of new information or ways to revise existing information. Remember that supporting information can include additional facts, precise details, and quotations. Try to include at least one quotation in your essay. Write your first draft and your revised draft on separate sheets of paper or in new documents.

**Conventions**

## Prepositions with Adjective and Adverb Phrases

**DIRECTIONS**  Look at the underlined prepositional phrases in each sentence. On the line, write *adjective* or *adverb* to identify the type of phrase. Then circle the word or words that the phrases modify.

1. This the oldest coin <u>in my collection</u>. _____

2. She walked <u>along the trail</u>. _____

3. Nick is sitting <u>between his parents</u> _____

4. The writer <u>from New York City</u> has just arrived. _____

5. The painting <u>on the wall</u> was a gift from my husband. _____

Students write routinely for a range of tasks, purposes, and audiences. Students practice various conventions of standard English.

Name _____

**DIRECTIONS** Write a sentence using each word.

legendary     occupied     bold     catastrophe

_____

_____

_____

_____

_____

_____

**Write in Response to Reading**

Reread pages 22–25. Write two paragraphs about the effects of the arrival of the British on the Aboriginal and the Torres Strait Islander peoples. Write your response below, on a separate sheet of paper, or in a new document.

_____

_____

_____

_____

_____

Students demonstrate contextual understanding of Benchmark Vocabulary. Students read text closely and use text evidence in their written answers.

## Relationships Between Individuals and Concepts

**DIRECTIONS** Using evidence from the text, answer the following questions about pages 16–19 of *Explorers: Triumphs and Troubles.*

1. What sparked the Spanish expedition through South America led by Gonzalo Pizarro?

   _____

   _____

   _____

2. What might have motivated Orellana, or his men, to continue downriver instead of returning to the rest of the group with the food they found?

   _____

   _____

   _____

3. What were the effects of Spanish exploration, including Orellana's journey, on the peoples of the Amazon region?

   _____

   _____

   _____

4. What other effect did Orellana's journey have? What specific event caused this effect?

   _____

   _____

   _____

 Students analyze and respond to literary and informational text.

**Add Transitions** Review your essay from Lesson 7. On a separate sheet of paper or in a new document, add or correct transitional words to make your reasoning clear. Remember to use transitions that match the organizational structure you have chosen for your essay.

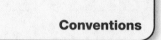

Conventions

## Conjunctions

**DIRECTIONS** Circle the conjunction that would best complete each sentence.

1. The Tlaxcalan people (and/or) the Spanish conquistadors attacked the Aztecs.

2. The Tibetans tried to fight off the British, (for/but) they realized they could not do it.

3. Marco Polo (and/nor) his father traveled on the Silk Road.

4. Exploring can be dangerous, (or/so) it is wise to be prepared.

5. Explorers in the Arctic had used sled dogs (and/nor) skis for many years, (for/yet) Robert Scott decided to use motorized sleds and ponies.

 Students write routinely for a range of tasks, purposes, and audiences. Students practice various conventions of standard English.

Name _____

**DIRECTIONS** Write a sentence using each word.

dedicate    capable    sullenly

_____

_____

_____

_____

**Write in Response to Reading**

Read the second paragraph on page 68. How would the feelings and ideas in the paragraph be different if it were written from the point of view of an observer on the dock? Write your response below, on a separate sheet of paper, or in a new document.

_____

_____

_____

_____

_____

Students demonstrate contextual understanding of Benchmark Vocabulary. Students read text closely and use text evidence in their written answers.

## Point of View

**DIRECTIONS** Using evidence from the text, answer the following questions about pages 68–73 of *Pedro's Journal*.

1. How does Pedro's description of his mother affect the reader's understanding of her character?

   _____

   _____

   _____

2. How do Pedro's journal entries affect the reader's understanding of the journey?

   _____

   _____

   _____

3. How does Pedro's description of the crew affect the reader's impression of the men working on the ship?

   _____

   _____

   _____

4. Write two sentences explaining how the reader's impression of the captain is influenced by Pedro.

   _____

   _____

   _____

Students analyze and respond to literary and informational text.

**Develop a Conclusion** Reread your revised essay, and draft your conclusion on a separate sheet of paper or in a new document. Team up with another student and review each other's conclusions. Ask your partner to check the following and provide feedback:

1. Does the conclusion restate the opinion given at the beginning of the essay?

2. Does the conclusion refer to the supporting evidence and reasons?

3. Does the conclusion include a final thought for the reader—something new that the writer has not yet mentioned?

Revise your conclusion based on feedback from you partner, if necessary.

**Conventions**

### Interjections

**DIRECTIONS** Underline the interjection that fits the emotion of the sentence.

1. (Oh no! / Wow!) The captain offered 10,000 maravedis to the first man to spot land.

2. (Hooray! / Oh no!) The food supplies and morale are running low.

3. (Oops! / Ugh!) I left the keys in the house.

4. (Hey! / Yikes!) You're not listening.

5. (Ugh! / Bravo!) I am so seasick.

Students write routinely for a range of tasks, purposes, and audiences. Students practice various conventions of standard English.

Name _____

**DIRECTIONS** Write a sentence using each word.

betrayal     assent     dispersed

_____

_____

_____

_____

**Write in Response to Reading**

Read page 77 of the entry for October 11. Write a paragraph analyzing the effects of descriptive details and dialogue on this page. Write your response below, on a separate sheet of paper, or in a new document.

_____

_____

_____

_____

_____

_____

Students demonstrate contextual understanding of Benchmark Vocabulary. Students read text closely and use text evidence in their written answers.

**Conduct Research**  Research multiple sources about Christopher Columbus. On a separate sheet of paper or in a new document, take notes on your findings using a variety of methods (paraphrasing, summarizing, and using direct quotes).

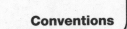

**Conventions**

## Correlative Conjunctions

**DIRECTIONS**  On the lines below, write three sentences using *either/or* and two sentences using *neither/nor*.

1. _____

   _____

2. _____

   _____

3. _____

   _____

4. _____

   _____

5. _____

   _____

 Students write routinely for a range of tasks, purposes, and audiences. Students practice various conventions of standard English.

## Compound Words

**DIRECTIONS** Combine two words from the Word Bank to form a compound word that will complete each sentence. You will use some words more than once.

### Word Bank

| hearted | fire | bound | place | clothes | night | over |
|---------|------|-------|-------|---------|--------|------|
| bells | coat | grand | out | side | mother | warm |
| doors | sleigh | book | story | snow | ball | in |
| shoes | pie | drifts | pot | storms | | |

1. An _____ is a great garment to wear on a chilly day.

2. Dana's _____ has an attic full of cold-weather gear.

3. Some of it is so old it could be from _____ times.

4. The _____, for example, could have been worn by explorers.

5. Horses wearing _____ could have trotted down snowy roads.

6. Families could have been _____ in their houses.

7. They would gather around the _____ and do projects.

8. Dana imagines pioneer women sewing _____ for the family.

9. Perhaps there would be a delicious _____ to eat.

10. Although snow fell _____, the family would be warm and dry.

11. Dana asks, "What did you do during _____, Nana?"

12. "Oh," she says, "we loved to have _____ fights!"

13. "We tunneled into _____ and built forts."

14. "Why didn't you huddle by the fire _____?" Dana asks.

15. "Playing was just too much fun," her _____ Nana says.

Students apply grade-level phonics and word analysis skills.

Name _____

**DIRECTIONS** Write a sentence using each word.

maneuvering    solemn    docile

_____

_____

_____

_____

**Write in Response to Reading**

Reread the paragraph on page 82. Use details from the text to write an opinion paragraph evaluating what Columbus and the crew members did to the native people. Write your response below, on a separate sheet of paper, or in a new document.

_____

_____

_____

_____

_____

Students demonstrate contextual understanding of Benchmark Vocabulary. Students read text closely and use text evidence in their written answers.

Name _____

**Synthesize Research** On a separate sheet of paper or in a new document, write a one-page opinion report about Christopher Columbus. Be sure to do the following:

1. Focus your research mainly on recent information about the explorer.

2. Use your research findings to develop and state an opinion.

3. Synthesize your research findings to support your stated opinion.

4. Include direct quotes, paraphrases, and summaries of your source material.

5. Credit your sources in a properly formatted Works Cited list.

**Conventions**

## Correlative Conjunctions

**DIRECTIONS** On the line, write the correlative conjunction that pairs correctly with the boldfaced word or words in the sentence.

1. _____ did the people smile at us **but** they **also** brought us gifts.

2. I had to **either** stay on the island _____ return to the ship.

3. We gave the people _____ beads **and** bells.

4. Pedro didn't know **whether** they would take native men back to Spain with them

   _____ if the men would all escape.

5. **Neither** Pedro _____ the other men expected the native people to appear.

Students write routinely for a range of tasks, purposes, and audiences. Students practice various conventions of standard English.

Name _____

**DIRECTIONS** Write a sentence using each word.

interpreter    meager    pompous

_____

_____

_____

_____

**Write in Response to Reading**

Use details from the book to write an informative paragraph explaining how characters' motivations help develop the theme, or message, of the text. Write your response below, on a separate sheet of paper, or in a new document.

_____

_____

_____

_____

_____

_____

Students demonstrate contextual understanding of Benchmark Vocabulary. Students read text closely and use text evidence in their written answers.

Name _____

## Character Motivation

**DIRECTIONS** Using evidence from the text, answer the following questions about page 84 from *Pedro's Journal*.

1. How does Pedro react to the news of a man's head being found in a basket? Why does he react this way?

_____

_____

_____

2. What does Columbus tell Diego to do? What can you infer about Diego from his response?

_____

_____

_____

3. What is the motivation of the group who join Pedro, Diego, Columbus, and the interpreter? How can you tell? Use examples from the text.

_____

_____

_____

_____

4. How do the interpreter and Columbus respond to the group's actions? Explain their reactions.

_____

_____

_____

_____

Students analyze and respond to literary and informational text.

**Plan an Opinion Essay**  Conduct research about how Columbus has been portrayed. Review the information presented in *Pedro's Journal* and at least two other sources. Then, on a separate sheet of paper or in a new document, write an opinion about how Columbus has been portrayed, and organize facts and evidence to support your opinion in an outline or graphic organizer. Remember to base your opinion on the facts and evidence you've gathered.

**Conventions**

## Independent and Dependent Clauses

**DIRECTIONS** Circle independent clauses and underline dependent clauses in the sentences below. Remember that independent clauses can be connected with the coordinating conjunctions *and, but, for, or, nor, so,* and *yet.*

1. When traveling from island to island, it is difficult to keep a journal.

2. There will always be some conflict during a long journey because people with different personalities are together for a long time.

3. Columbus tried to trade with the native people, but they did not trust him.

4. He laughed at the native people after they ran away.

5. Columbus was arrogant, and his translator was cautious.

Students write routinely for a range of tasks, purposes, and audiences. Students practice various conventions of standard English.

Name _____

**DIRECTIONS** Write a sentence using each word.

distract    enchanted    striving

_____

_____

_____

**Write in Response to Reading**

Read the second sentence in the entry on page 90. Write a paragraph discussing how the imagery and figurative language in this sentence appeals to the senses of hearing, touch, and sight. Write your response below, on a separate sheet of paper, or in a new document.

_____

_____

_____

_____

_____

Students demonstrate contextual understanding of Benchmark Vocabulary. Students read text closely and use text evidence in their written answers.

## Pants with History

Did you know those denim pants you see everywhere are part of American history? This is the story of how two hardworking and creative immigrants came together to produce the first blue jeans.

In 1848, a young German named Loeb Strauss immigrated to New York with his mother and two sisters. His older brothers owned a company that sold fabric and clothing there. After gold was discovered in California, Strauss saw it as a business opportunity. Gold was a valuable resource. Some gold prospectors "struck it rich." Many other people grew wealthy providing the more mundane goods and services to the miners and other California settlers. In 1853, young Strauss, now called Levi, traveled to California. He began distributing his brothers' fabric and clothing.

Contrary to popular myth, however, Levi Strauss did not invent the blue jeans known as "Levi's." Born in Latvia (LAT-vee-uh), Jacob Davis was a tailor who made clothing. He also made items like horse blankets. The demand for heavy-duty work clothes grew. Davis, who lived in Nevada, began making "waist-high overalls" from cotton duck fabric, which is like canvas. He purchased the cotton duck from Strauss. The term blue jeans comes from a fabric called "jean." It is much like denim and was used to make pants in the nineteenth century.

Because thread alone wasn't strong enough to fasten the pockets onto the pants, Jacob decided to add copper rivets. He had successfully used rivets on horse blankets. As the durable pants became more popular with miners, ranchers, and farmers, Davis decided to obtain a patent. In 1872, he wrote to Strauss. He offered to share the rights to the riveting process if Strauss would help mass market the product.

Strauss then brought Davis to San Francisco to supervise the manufacture of riveted jeans by Levi Strauss & Co. On May 20, 1873, the patent was granted. That day is considered the official birthday of blue jeans. The pants soon became a best seller. Straus and Davis had struck "blue gold."

 Students read text closely to determine what the text says.

**Gather Evidence** Underline the event that inspired Levi Strauss to move away from his family and strike out on his own.

**Gather Evidence: Extend Your Ideas** Write the activities of others that encouraged Strauss as he began his new business.

_____

_____

_____

**Ask Questions** Write two questions you would ask Levi Strauss and Jacob Davis about challenges they faced.

_____

_____

_____

**Ask Questions: Extend Your Ideas** Write an additional question about challenges that is answered in the text. Underline the answer in the text.

_____

_____

**Make Your Case** List the contributions each partner made to the development of blue jeans.

_____

_____

_____

**Make Your Case: Extend Your Ideas** Who was more instrumental in the eventual worldwide success of blue jeans, Strauss or Davis? Discuss your results with a partner.

_____

_____

 Students read text closely to determine what the text says.

Name _____

**Draft an Opinion Essay** Write a first draft of your opinion essay. Base your essay on the following prompt: Based on what you know and have read about Christopher Columbus, do you think Columbus is portrayed fairly in *Pedro's Journal*? Use the outline or graphic organizer you created in Lesson 12 as a guide as you develop your draft. Write your draft on a separate sheet of paper or in a new document.

**Conventions**

## Connecting Independent Clauses

**DIRECTIONS** Connect the two independent clauses in each item with the best coordinating conjunction: *and, but, so, or* or *yet*. Use each conjunction only once.

1. I wanted to sleep in this morning, _____ the crew had too much work to do.

2. We could stop at the island that the man mentioned, _____ we could sail home.

3. I could not sleep, _____ I decided to get up.

4. I went onto the deck, _____ I found the captain alone there.

5. I was eager to go on this voyage, _____ I don't want to go on another one.

Students write routinely for a range of tasks, purposes, and audiences. Students practice various conventions of standard English.

Name _____

**DIRECTIONS** Write a sentence using each word.

pompous    bold

_____

_____

_____

_____

**Write in Response to Reading**

Write a paragraph that explains how the text structure of either *Explorers: Triumphs and Troubles* or *Pedro's Journal* helps the reader better understand the author's purpose. Cite text evidence to support your response. Write your response below, on a separate sheet of paper, or in a new document.

_____

_____

_____

_____

_____

_____

Students demonstrate contextual understanding of Benchmark Vocabulary. Students read text closely and use text evidence in their written answers.

**Unit 4 • Module A • Lesson 14 • 349**

**Revise and Rewrite** Pair up with another student, and review his or her essay, suggesting revisions and rewrites. Check for the following:

1. The opinion statement is clear and supported with reasons and evidence.

2. The sentence structure is effective, and the writer uses parallel structure.

3. The writer uses precise, specific language instead of vague, general words.

4. The organization of ideas is logical, and transitions make clear connections between ideas and paragraphs.

After reviewing your partner's draft, revise or rewrite parts of your essay as needed based on the comments you receive. Use a separate sheet of paper or start a new document.

**Conventions**

## Use Subordinating Conjunctions

**DIRECTIONS** Write five sentences that include a subordinating conjunction. Underline the independent clause and circle the dependent clause in each sentence.

1. _____

_____

2. _____

_____

3. _____

_____

4. _____

_____

5. _____

_____

 Students write routinely for a range of tasks, purposes, and audiences. Students practice various conventions of standard English.

**DIRECTIONS** Write a sentence using each word.

advantage    immensity    solitude    unison

_____

_____

_____

_____

_____

**Write in Response to Reading**

Based on Ría's and Derrick's actions, are Brandon's opinions of them fair and accurate? Support your opinion with evidence from the text. Write your response below, on a separate sheet of paper, or in a new document.

_____

_____

_____

_____

_____

Students demonstrate contextual understanding of Benchmark Vocabulary. Students read text closely and use text evidence in their written answers.

Name _____

## Point of View

**DIRECTIONS** Using evidence from the text, answer the following questions about pages 91–93 from "Secrets of the Canyon Cave."

1. What are Brandon's feelings about the scavenger hunt?

   _____

   _____

2. How does the reader know how Brandon feels about the scavenger hunt? Use evidence from the text to explain your answer.

   _____

   _____

   _____

   _____

3. How does Brandon feel about their decision to use the route he chose?

   _____

   _____

4. How does the reader know that Brandon feels this way? Use evidence from the text to explain your answer.

   _____

   _____

   _____

   _____

Students analyze and respond to literary and informational text.

**Edit and Proofread an Opinion Essay** Exchange drafts with a partner who did not review your draft in Lesson 14, and review his or her revised draft to check for proper grammar, usage, spelling, punctuation, and capitalization. Remember to create and use a checklist to check for conventions covered in this module. After you and your partner have edited each other's work, incorporate your partner's edits into your essay. Create a clean final draft on a separate sheet of paper or in a new document.

**Conventions**

### Correcting Sentence Fragments

**DIRECTIONS** On the line next to each item from pages 93 and 95 of "Secrets of the Canyon Cave," write *S* if the word group is a sentence and *F* if the word group is not a sentence. If it is a fragment, rewrite it to create a complete sentence.

1. In unison with nature. _____.

2. In a word—incredible. _____.

3. Brandon couldn't believe their luck. _____.

4. "Go that way." _____.

5. A cave dwelling? _____.

 Students write routinely for a range of tasks, purposes, and audiences. Students practice various conventions of standard English.

## Words from Russian

**DIRECTIONS**  In each sentence below, a word from Russian is misspelled.
Write the correct spelling on the line.

1. The babooshka is a very warm scarf. _____

2. The animal known as the sabel is sleek and brown. _____

3. Nicholas was the last Russian zar. _____

4. A head covering with eyeholes might be a baklava. _____

5. Outside of Moscow there were many dakkas. _____

6. Often, the baluga whale is nearly white. _____

7. Tea from a semmivor tastes special. _____

8. One Russian instrument is called a balalalaka. _____

9. Many mamoths lived in grasslands. _____

10. The cahzmonaut stayed in space for a year. _____

11. Tunder is a cold area of the world. _____

12. If you have beets in your garden, make borst. _____

13. Many fir trees grow in the area called tagai. _____

14. A jacket with a furry hood might be a praka. _____

15. The steps are a kind of Russian grassland. _____

 Students apply grade-level phonics and word
analysis skills.

**DIRECTIONS** Write a sentence using each word.

unfurled     detected     interconnected     ingenious

_____

_____

_____

_____

_____

**Write in Response to Reading**

Use descriptive details about the "ancient device" Ría and Brandon discovered to write an informative paragraph about what it looked like, how it was designed, and how it worked. Write your response below, on a separate sheet of paper, or in a new document.

_____

_____

_____

_____

_____

_____

Students demonstrate contextual understanding of Benchmark Vocabulary. Students read text closely and use text evidence in their written answers.

**Publish and Present an Opinion Essay**  Your teacher will divide your class into two groups according to the opinions expressed about Christopher Columbus in Lesson 12. With your group, plan and then engage in a debate, which should consist of the following:

1. An opening argument, in which each group presents its opinion and supports it with reasons and evidence

2. A response to the opposing group's counterarguments

3. A closing statement, in which each group summarizes its main points

All students in your group should participate in planning the group's argument and should have a chance to speak during the debate. Take notes on your group's plan for the debate on a separate sheet of paper or in a new document.

**Conventions**

## Correct Run-On Sentences

**DIRECTIONS**  Correct each run-on sentence below by creating two sentences, by using a semicolon, and by using a coordinating conjunction.

**They found shelter in a cave, they spent the night.**

1. _____

2. _____

3. _____

**The clouds cleared, the stars were visible.**

4. _____

5. _____

6. _____

 Students write routinely for a range of tasks, purposes, and audiences. Students practice various conventions of standard English.

Name _____

**DIRECTIONS** Write a sentence using each word.

various     generation     disgrace

_____

_____

_____

_____

**Write in Response to Reading**

In "Turtle's Race with Bear," who responds more effectively to the situation—Turtle or Bear? Write an opinion paragraph citing details from the text to support your answer. Write your response below, on a separate sheet of paper, or in a new document.

_____

_____

_____

_____

_____

Students demonstrate contextual understanding of Benchmark Vocabulary. Students read text closely and use text evidence in their written answers.

Name _____

## Compare and Contrast Responses to Events

**DIRECTIONS** Using evidence from the texts, answer the following questions about "Turtle's Race with Bear" and "How the Butterflies Came to Be."

1. How does Turtle respond when Bear calls him "Slow One"?

_____

_____

2. During his race with Turtle, how does Bear respond to what is happening? What does he do after the race is over?

_____

_____

_____

3. How do the songbirds respond to Elder Brother's action?

_____

_____

4. How does Elder Brother respond to the songbirds?

_____

_____

5. How are the characters in the stories alike and different in the way they respond to being offended or learning a lesson?

_____

_____

_____

 Students analyze and respond to literary and informational text.

**Plan an Opinion Essay** Plan an opinion essay that responds to the following prompt: Determine the most important theme or issue that the texts in the module reveal about the experience of exploration. On a separate sheet of paper or in a new document, write a clear opinion statement. Then create an outline that lists reasons and evidence from the texts in the module. Use either a block or point-by-point organizational structure.

**Conventions**

## Spell Correctly

**DIRECTIONS** Carefully read each word below, and rewrite it spelled correctly.

1. peice _____

2. cieling _____

3. feild _____

4. freind _____

5. reciept _____

6. wierd _____

 Students write routinely for a range of tasks, purposes, and audiences. Students practice various conventions of standard English.

Name _____

**DIRECTIONS** Write a sentence using each word.

limitless    ambition    enchanted    immensity    solitude

_____

_____

_____

_____

_____

_____

_____

**Write in Response to Reading**

Use details from all three texts to write an informative paragraph about some of the tools explorers use. Write your response below, on a separate sheet of paper, or in a new document.

_____

_____

_____

_____

_____

_____

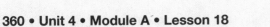

Students demonstrate contextual understanding of Benchmark Vocabulary. Students read text closely and use text evidence in their written answers.

Name _____

**Draft and Revise an Opinion Essay** Draft and revise your opinion essay based on the outline you prepared in Lesson 17. Write your draft and revision on separate sheets of paper or in new documents.

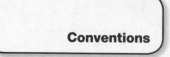

**Conventions**

## Spell Correctly

**DIRECTIONS** Carefully read each word below, and rewrite it spelled correctly.

1. latly _____

2. noteable _____

3. exciteing _____

4. placment _____

5. createion _____

6. responseible _____

 Students write routinely for a range of tasks, purposes, and audiences. Students practice various conventions of standard English.

## Complex Spelling Patterns

**DIRECTIONS** From each set of words, choose the one in which the letters *ci* or *ti* spell the /sh/ sound or the letters *ous* spell the /əs/ sound. Write the word on the line.

_____ 1. positive / position / possible

_____ 2. house / momentous / trousers

_____ 3. fraction / plentiful / festive

_____ 4. slicing / glacier / recite

_____ 5. grouse / roustabout / fabulous

_____ 6. tactical / spatial / effective

_____ 7. acoustic / hilarious / joust

_____ 8. mousse / blouse / curious

_____ 9. society / physician / prettily

_____ 10. retaliation / creative / retinue

_____ 11. devious / rousing / thousand

_____ 12. mention / politics / reptilian

_____ 13. anonymous / lousy / ouster

_____ 14. retired / convertible / dictionary

_____ 15. scientist / especially / cicada

Students apply grade-level phonics and word analysis skills.

Name _____

**DIRECTIONS** Write a sentence using each word.

wager    wondrous    barbarous    pondered

_____

_____

_____

_____

_____

**Write in Response to Reading**

Read pages 4–7. Use details from the text to write a paragraph describing two ways that Sarah and her father are alike and two ways that they are different. Write your response below, on a separate sheet of paper, or in a new document.

_____

_____

_____

_____

_____

_____

Students demonstrate contextual understanding of Benchmark Vocabulary. Students read text closely and use text evidence in their written answers.

**Choose an Issue** Choose an issue related to *Beyond the Horizon*, such as whether expanding trade during the Age of Exploration was worth the consequences to explorers and the people they encountered in other lands. Then write a one-paragraph summary of the issue from the point of view of someone living during the 1500s who has experience exploring or with explorers. This point of view will help you choose the tone and language you will use throughout your editorial. Write your summary on a separate sheet of paper or in a new document.

**Conventions**

### Subject-Verb Agreement: Compound Subjects

**DIRECTIONS** Write five sentences that have compound subjects. Make sure that the verb agrees with the compound subject.

1. _____

   _____

2. _____

   _____

3. _____

   _____

4. _____

   _____

5. _____

   _____

 Students write routinely for a range of tasks, purposes, and audiences. Students practice various conventions of standard English.

**DIRECTIONS** Write a sentence using each word.

verdict    mate    sustenance    treaty

_____

_____

_____

_____

_____

_____

**Write in Response to Reading**

Read paragraphs three through five on page 20. Use text details to infer what causes Sarah to realize why Captain Booth had tried to protect her from the journey to India. Write your response below, on a separate sheet of paper, or in a new document.

_____

_____

_____

_____

_____

_____

Students demonstrate contextual understanding of Benchmark Vocabulary. Students read text closely and use text evidence in their written answers.

## Make Inferences About Causes

**DIRECTIONS** Using evidence from the text, answer the following questions about pages 12–18 from *Beyond the Horizon*.

1. Based on text details, what inference can you make about why the cook decides to hire Sarah?

   _____

   _____

   _____

2. What text details did you use to make your inference about why the cook decides to hire Sarah?

   _____

   _____

   _____

3. What inference can you make about why Sarah does not look directly at Captain Booth as she brings the tray of food to him and Lieutenant Armitage?

   _____

   _____

   _____

4. What text details did you use to make your inference about why Sarah does not look directly at Captain Booth?

   _____

   _____

   _____

Students analyze and respond to literary and informational text.

**Gather Evidence for an Editorial** First, follow the steps Reread, Weigh, and Decide to determine your opinion on your chosen issue. Then, on separate sheets of paper or in a new document, write two pages of notes for your editorial. State your opinion, identify three strong reasons that support your opinion, and identify text evidence from *Beyond the Horizon* that supports your reasons.

**Conventions**

### Subject-Verb Agreement: Compound Verbs

**DIRECTIONS** Write five sentences that feature compound verbs. Make sure that the compound verbs agree with the subject.

1. _____

   _____

2. _____

   _____

3. _____

   _____

4. _____

   _____

5. _____

   _____

Students write routinely for a range of tasks, purposes, and audiences. Students practice various conventions of standard English.

Name _____

**DIRECTIONS** Write a sentence using each word.

berth    barrows    pungent    bullock

_____

_____

_____

_____

_____

_____

**Write in Response to Reading**

Read pages 26–27. Retell the sequence of story events from the point of view of Tom the cat. Write your response below, on a separate sheet of paper, or in a new document.

_____

_____

_____

_____

_____

Students demonstrate contextual understanding of Benchmark Vocabulary. Students read text closely and use text evidence in their written answers.

**This Is the Place**

"I can't believe that we finally made it, Father. What an arduous journey! The mountains, the rivers, the buffalo herds, and the weather —I've had enough!" exclaimed Rebecca.

"Indeed, Rebecca. We have endured many hardships, but seeing this great expanse of land and knowing that our pioneer brothers and sisters are here, I feel relieved."

Rebecca and her family had traveled for months, along with hundreds of other Mormons, to the Salt Lake Valley. They had no idea that the first Mormon settlement, in Nauvoo, Illinois, would not be permanent.

Rebecca sighed, and wrapped her arms around her twin sisters. "At least we are together and no one perished." She looked all around and breathed in the clear, cleansing air. "This land seems so peaceful and safe, unlike Nauvoo. I just hope this valley does not bring us the same circumstances. It was so unfair how people treated us there!" Rebecca cried, and abruptly sat down on a rock.

"We may always feel persecuted, Rebecca, you must understand that. This is why Brigham Young has led us west, far away from other settlements, so that we can worship freely—and without human judgment," explained her father.

"I wonder how Mr. Young knew that this valley would be a safe haven for us?" wondered Rebecca. She rose from the rock and squinted at the blazing sun.

"He is a wise man, a true follower of the faith, and a fearless leader, Rebecca. When he arrived here, Young said, 'This is the place, drive on,'" added her father.

Rebecca replied, "I am thankful, Papa, that we have a new home and a place to practice our religion and way of life without being ridiculed, yet I do miss our home back east. I yearn to see my friends and my school."

Rebecca's father shook his head and approached Rebecca. "I understand, but your school and your friends' families, all of them thought of you differently because you are Mormon."

"You're right, Papa, but it's just not fair. How could our countrymen, who came to this land to seek religious freedom, practice such hypocrisy?" argued Rebecca. Rebecca stomped away, kicking dirt with her tattered boots to release some aggression. She sat down on the back of the wagon to gather her thoughts. Her father pushed a wooden chest out of the way and sat next to her. He wiped Rebecca's hair away from her weary face and prayed.

Students read text closely to determine what the text says.

**Gather Evidence**  Underline the main reason that Rebecca and her family moved to Salt Lake Valley. Add brackets around the hardships Rebecca and her family experienced on their journey west.



**Gather Evidence: Extend Your Ideas**  Review the text details you underlined and bracketed. What conclusion can you draw about how the family responds to challenges?

_____

_____

**Ask Questions**  Write two questions you would ask Rebecca about her experiences in Nauvoo.

_____

_____

**Ask Questions: Extend Your Ideas**  List an additional question about Rebecca's life in Nauvoo that is answered in the text. Place a box around the answer in the text.

_____

_____

**Make Your Case**  In what time period does this story take place? Circle clues in the text that relate to the time period.



**Make Your Case: Extend Your Ideas**  How does knowing the time period of the story help you better understand the events in it? Discuss your ideas with a partner.

_____

_____

 Students read text closely to determine what the text says.

**Organize Reasons and Evidence for an Editorial** Develop an outline that shows a logical organization for your editorial. Remember to use your notes to add relevant facts and details to the "Supporting Evidence" parts of your outline. Write your outline on a separate sheet of paper or in a new document.

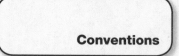

**Conventions**

### Subject-Verb Agreement: Phrases

**DIRECTIONS** On the lines in items 1–5, write original sentences in which prepositional phrases or other types of phrases appear between the subject and the verb. Make sure that the subject and verb agree in number.

1. _____

    _____

2. _____

    _____

3. _____

    _____

4. _____

    _____

5. _____

    _____

Students write routinely for a range of tasks, purposes, and audiences. Students practice various conventions of standard English.

Name _____

**DIRECTIONS** Write a sentence using each word.

tidings    anguish    channel    silhouette

_____

_____

_____

_____

_____

_____

**Write in Response to Reading**

Read page 37. Write a paragraph describing how the author's word choice and sentence structure convey Sarah's physical pain and emotional state to the reader. Write your response below, on a separate sheet of paper, or in a new document.

_____

_____

_____

_____

_____

Students demonstrate contextual understanding of Benchmark Vocabulary. Students read text closely and use text evidence in their written answers.

Name _____

**Strengthen Reasons and Evidence in an Editorial** Write a draft of your editorial. Remember that you are writing from the point of view of someone living in the 1500s and that your audience is people living in the 1500s. As you draft, keep in mind your purpose, too: to persuade your audience that exploration is or is not worth it and should or should not be undertaken. Write your draft on a separate sheet of paper or in a new document.

**Conventions**

## Subject-Verb Agreement: Indefinite Pronouns

**DIRECTIONS** Write five sentences that feature indefinite pronouns as subjects. Make sure that the subject and verb agree in number.

1. _____

_____

2. _____

_____

3. _____

_____

4. _____

_____

5. _____

_____

Students write routinely for a range of tasks, purposes, and audiences. Students practice various conventions of standard English.

Name _____

**DIRECTIONS** Write a sentence using each word.

tethered     lilting

_____

_____

_____

_____

**Write in Response to Reading**

Read pages 44–47 and review the illustrations. Then write a paragraph explaining how the text structure and the illustrations in this section work together to help readers understand what is happening in the story. Write your response below, on a separate sheet of paper, or in a new document.

_____

_____

_____

_____

_____

Students demonstrate contextual understanding of Benchmark Vocabulary. Students read text closely and use text evidence in their written answers.

## Lesson 5

**Language Analysis**

Name _____

## Text Structure and Text Features

**DIRECTIONS** Using evidence from the text, answer the following questions about pages 40–47 from *Beyond the Horizon*.

1. How is the text in this section structured?

   _____

   _____

2. What words and phrases from the text serve as clues to the text's structure?

   _____

   _____

   _____

   _____

   _____

3. What event from the story does the illustration on page 45 relate to?

   _____

   _____

   _____

4. How does the illustration on page 45 help you better understand the story?

   _____

   _____

   _____

Students analyze and respond to literary and informational text.

Name _____

**Develop Appropriate Tone and Voice in an Editorial** Exchange editorial drafts with a partner and follow the steps below to conduct a peer review and revise your draft.

1. Evaluate whether the tone is appropriate for the purpose and the audience, and whether your partner chose words and phrases that develop a natural and individual voice.

2. Identify ways to revise sentences to develop an engaging, effective, and interesting voice. Suggest various techniques, such as parallelism, rhetorical questions, and repetition, where appropriate.

3. Revise your draft based on your partner's feedback. Use a separate sheet of paper or start a new document.

**Conventions**

## Subject-Verb Agreement: Collective Nouns

**DIRECTIONS** Underline the collective noun in each sentence. Then use context to determine whether the collective noun should take a singular or plural verb, and write *singular* or *plural* on the line. Finally, circle the verb form that correctly completes the sentence.

1. The audience (applaud / applauds) at the end of the performance. _____

2. One by one, the group (arrive / arrives) at the destination. _____

3. The team (practice / practices) every day after school. _____

4. The family (take / takes) turns weeding the garden. _____

5. The committee (give / gives) a presentation at the conference. _____

 Students write routinely for a range of tasks, purposes, and audiences. Students practice various conventions of standard English.

## Word Families

**DIRECTIONS** For each word family, identify the base word and write it on the line.

_____ 1. marvelous, marveling, marveled

_____ 2. breakable, unbroken, breaker

_____ 3. reclaim, disclaimer, unclaimed

_____ 4. personality, personable, personify

_____ 5. astonishing, astonishment, astonished

_____ 6. darken, darkly, semidarkness

_____ 7. speedy, speeding, speediest

_____ 8. watchful, unwatchable, watching

_____ 9. useful, misuse, uselessly

_____ 10. growth, grower, outgrow

**DIRECTIONS** Read each base word and its definition. Then write a word that belongs in the same word family.

11. imagine: to picture in one's mind _____

12. blend: to thoroughly mix together _____

13. year: a period of 365 days _____

14. fragrance: a pleasant odor _____

15. regret: to feel sorry or disappointed _____

16. choose: to select _____

17. take: to get possession of _____

18. place: an area of space with boundaries _____

19. little: small in size or amount _____

20. good: positive _____

Students apply grade-level phonics and word analysis skills.

Name _____

**DIRECTIONS** Write a sentence using each word.

anchorage    tarry    imploring

_____

_____

_____

_____

_____

**Write in Response to Reading**

Read pages 54–55. Write a paragraph describing the effect that the arrival of the two ships has on the people of the village, as well the effect it has on Sarah. Write your response below, on a separate sheet of paper, or in a new document.

_____

_____

_____

_____

_____

Students demonstrate contextual understanding of Benchmark Vocabulary. Students read text closely and use text evidence in their written answers.

**Address Opposing Viewpoints in an Editorial** Revise your editorial to include an opposing viewpoint. First, anticipate an opposing viewpoint, and take notes about how to address it. Address and refute the opposing viewpoint in a way that connects back to and strengthens your own opinion. Next, determine the best place in your body paragraphs to include your response to an opposing viewpoint. Think of transitions to use to move easily from the opposing viewpoint to your own opinion and make your thinking clear to the reader. Finally, revise your editorial to include your response to an opposing viewpoint. Keep your purpose (to persuade) and your audience (people in the 1500s) in mind as you revise your editorial. Use a separate sheet of paper or start a new document.

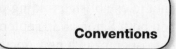

**Conventions**

## Subject-Verb Agreement: Collective Nouns

**DIRECTIONS** Circle the collective nouns in each sentence. Use the context of the sentence to determine whether the collective noun is singular or plural. On the line, write the correct form of the verb in parentheses.

1. The family _____ firewood for the campfire. (collect)

2. The class _____ the museum on a field trip. (visit)

3. One at a time, the group _____ their views. (express)

4. At the beginning of practice, the team _____ laps. (run)

5. The scientific committee _____ on the study results. (disagree)

 Students write routinely for a range of tasks, purposes, and audiences. Students practice various conventions of standard English.

Name _____

**DIRECTIONS** Write a sentence using each word.

precaution    regardless    fate    revelation

_____

_____

_____

_____

_____

**Write in Response to Reading**

Read pages 56–61. Write a paragraph describing what causes Captain Booth to decide not to establish a trading post in the village and the effect this decision appears to have on both Sarah and Lieutenant Armitage. Write your response below, on a separate sheet of paper, or in a new document.

_____

_____

_____

_____

_____

Students demonstrate contextual understanding of Benchmark Vocabulary. Students read text closely and use text evidence in their written answers.

## Cause-Effect Relationships

**DIRECTIONS** Using evidence from the text, answer the following questions about pages 56–64 from *Beyond the Horizon*.

1. How do the villagers respond when they see the sailors at the top of the hill? What does this response cause Captain Booth to do?

   _____

   _____

   _____

2. Why does Captain Booth tell his men to lower their weapons and not confront the villagers? Cite specific details from the text to support your response.

   _____

   _____

   _____

   _____

   _____

3. How does visiting Priya's family affect Captain Booth? Support your response with text evidence.

   _____

   _____

   _____

   _____

   _____

Students analyze and respond to literary and informational text.

**Add Transitions in an Editorial** Exchange editorial drafts with a partner. Review your partner's draft, looking for unclear organization and points where the connections between the reasons, supporting evidence, and the opinion statement are either confusing or absent. Suggest transitions to clarify and strengthen the connections between the reasons and the opinion statement and between the reasons and the supporting evidence. Revise your draft based on your partner's feedback. Use a separate sheet of paper or start a new document.

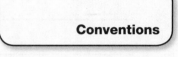

**Conventions**

## Subject-Verb Agreement: Hard-to-Find Subjects

**DIRECTIONS** Underline the subject in each sentence. Then circle the verb that correctly completes the sentence.

1. On a hill near the village (stands / stand) the men with their weapons.

2. There (is / are) a group of villagers standing at the bottom of the hill.

3. There (is / are) sailors prepared to attack them.

4. Beneath the villagers' fierce exteriors (beats / beat) brave hearts.

5. There (is / are) many reasons the villagers want to protect their homes.

 Students write routinely for a range of tasks, purposes, and audiences. Students practice various conventions of standard English.

## Lesson 8

Name _____

**DIRECTIONS** Write a sentence using each word.

sustenance    provisions    peasants    wielding    grudgingly

_____

_____

_____

_____

_____

_____

_____

**Write in Response to Reading**

Read pages 4–7 in Chapter 1. Write a paragraph describing how the text structure on these pages helps to introduce the main characters and set up the story's central conflicts. Write your response below, on a separate sheet of paper, or in a new document.

_____

_____

_____

_____

_____

Students demonstrate contextual understanding of Benchmark Vocabulary. Students read text closely and use text evidence in their written answers.

**Develop a Conclusion in an Editorial** On a separate sheet of paper or in a new document, draft the conclusion to your editorial. Summarize the opinion and the main points of the editorial, and provide an answer or a solution to the issue presented in the editorial. Once you have finished writing your conclusion, exchange drafts with a partner for peer review. Comment on your partner's conclusion in pencil, or use sticky notes for suggestions. Then revise your draft based on your partner's feedback.

Conventions

## Punctuating Items in a Series: Commas

**DIRECTIONS** Combine the sentences in each item into one sentence, using commas to separate words, phrases, or clauses in a series.

1. Sarah wore Henry's shoes. Sarah wore Henry's doublet. Sarah wore Henry's cap.

   _____

2. The sailors ate salted beef. The sailors ate hardtack. The sailors ate cheese.

   _____

3. The ship sailed across the sea. The ship sailed along the coast. The ship sailed

   into port. _____

   _____

4. Sailors who worked hard were valued. Sailors who were strong were valued. Sailors who could endure hardships were valued.

   _____

   _____

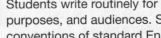
Students write routinely for a range of tasks, purposes, and audiences. Students practice various conventions of standard English.

Name _____

**DIRECTIONS** Write a sentence using the word.

voyage

_____

_____

_____

_____

**Write in Response to Reading**

Read Chapter 1 and review the text features. Which text feature does the best job of supporting the main text? Use evidence from the text in your response. Write your response below, on a separate sheet of paper, or in a new document.

_____

_____

_____

_____

_____

_____

Students demonstrate contextual understanding of Benchmark Vocabulary. Students read text closely and use text evidence in their written answers.

## Visual Elements

**DIRECTIONS** Using evidence from the text, answer the following questions about Chapter 1 of *Explorers of North America*.

1. List one fact the author states on page 9.

   _____

   _____

   _____

2. How does the map on page 8 support that point?

   _____

   _____

   _____

3. How does the map support the author's point that the Vikings were known for their sailing skills?

   _____

   _____

   _____

4. How does the map's caption support the author's point that the Vikings were known for their sailing skills?

   _____

   _____

   _____

Students analyze and respond to literary and informational text.

Name _____

**Revise Drafts**  Revise your editorial draft. Put all the pieces of your editorial draft together in order, using the checklist reviewed during the lesson as a guide to rearrange and cut or revise as needed. Review a partner's draft to identify any gaps, weaknesses, or issues with tone. Then revise your draft based on your partner's feedback on a separate sheet of paper or in a new document.

## Punctuating Items in a Series: Semicolons

**DIRECTIONS**  Write a sentence to answer each question. Include at least three items in each response. Briefly describe each item that you list, using a comma to set off the description from the item. Use semicolons to separate the items in your list.

1. Where are three places in the world that you would like to visit someday?

   _____

   _____

   _____

2. What are your favorite books, and what are they about?

   _____

   _____

   _____

Students write routinely for a range of tasks, purposes, and audiences. Students practice various conventions of standard English.

**DIRECTIONS** Write a sentence using the word.

expensive

_____

_____

_____

_____

**Write in Response to Reading**

Read page 11. Then use text evidence to write an informative paragraph about the dangers faced by traders who used the Silk Road. Write your response below, on a separate sheet of paper, or in a new document.

_____

_____

_____

_____

_____

 Students demonstrate contextual understanding of Benchmark Vocabulary. Students read text closely and use text evidence in their written answers.

**Conduct Research** Choose one of the explorers you have read about in Unit 4. Research multiple print and digital sources to find information about how your chosen explorer prepared for his or her journey. Take notes and record source information as you research. Remember that any words copied directly from a source should appear in quotation marks and should be followed by a page reference. Write your research notes on a separate sheet of paper or in a new document.

**Conventions**

## Commas and Introductory Elements

**DIRECTIONS** Use each prompt below to write a sentence that includes an introductory word or phrase set off by a comma.

1. Tell when European traders journeyed to Asia and why they made the journey.

   _____

   _____

2. Tell how Christopher Columbus was unlike other explorers of the time.

   _____

   _____

3. Tell when John Cabot and his crew began their second journey to find Asia, and what happened to them.

   _____

   _____

   _____

 Students write routinely for a range of tasks, purposes, and audiences. Students practice various conventions of standard English.

Name _____

## Compound Words

**DIRECTIONS** Draw a line between the smaller words in each compound word. Then write the smaller words on the line.

_____     1.  breathtaking

_____     2.  nonetheless

_____     3.  faceoff

_____     4.  powerboat

_____     5.  paperweight

_____     6.  afterthought

_____     7.  workstation

_____     8.  cartwheel

_____     9.  sinkhole

_____     10. counterclockwise

**DIRECTIONS** Each compound word below has a meaning that cannot be determined from the meanings of the smaller words it contains. Using a dictionary or glossary as needed, write a sentence for each word that reveals its meaning.

11.  dashboard _____

12.  backlog _____

13.  playbill _____

14.  sidestep _____

15.  brainchild _____

 Students apply grade-level phonics and word analysis skills.

Name _____

**DIRECTIONS** Write a sentence using each word.

capital     victory

_____

_____

_____

_____

**Write in Response to Reading**

Read the first paragraph on page 19. Write an opinion paragraph about Cortés's actions, using text evidence and reasons to support your opinion. Write your response below, on a separate sheet of paper, or in a new document.

_____

_____

_____

_____

_____

_____

Students demonstrate contextual understanding of Benchmark Vocabulary. Students read text closely and use text evidence in their written answers.

**Synthesize Research**  On a separate sheet of paper or in a new document, write a report, one to two pages long, that synthesizes your findings about how your chosen explorer prepared for a voyage. In addition, prepare a Works Cited page that lists all your sources.

**Conventions**

## Commas with Introductory Elements

**DIRECTIONS**  On the line below each prompt, write a sentence to respond to the prompt. Begin each sentence with a time-related introductory adverb phrase.

1. Think about a fun activity you did recently. Write when it happened and what it was.

   _____

   _____

2. Think about a time when you helped someone. Write when it happened and what it was.

   _____

   _____

3. Think about a time when someone helped you. Write when it happened and what it was.

   _____

   _____

4. Think about a time when you learned an important lesson. Write when it happened and what it was.

   _____

   _____

 Students write routinely for a range of tasks, purposes, and audiences. Students practice various conventions of standard English.

Name _____

**DIRECTIONS** Write a sentence using each word.

rebelled    intentions

_____
_____
_____
_____

**Write in Response to Reading**

Read the second paragraph on page 28. Use details from the chapter to write an explanatory paragraph about why the British government offered a cash prize. Write your response below, on a separate sheet of paper, or in a new document.

_____
_____
_____
_____
_____
_____

Students demonstrate contextual understanding of Benchmark Vocabulary. Students read text closely and use text evidence in their written answers.

Name _____

## Main Ideas and Key Details

**DIRECTIONS** Using evidence from the text, answer the following questions about Chapter 4 of *Explorers of North America*.

1. What is one main idea of the section "Rebellion on the *Discovery*" on pages 26–27?

   _____

   _____

   _____

2. What two details from the text support the main idea you identified in question 2?

   _____

   _____

   _____

3. What is one main idea of the section "Cook Tries Another Route" on pages 28–29?

   _____

   _____

   _____

4. Cite two pieces of text evidence to support the main idea you identified in question 4.

   _____

   _____

   _____

Students analyze and respond to literary and informational text.

Name _____

**Plan an Editorial** Write an opinion statement based upon this prompt: *Many explorers didn't find what they were looking for, but they made other important discoveries. Imagine you are a British explorer in the late 1700s inspired by James Cook's story. Write an editorial urging the British government to fund your mission despite Cook's tragedy.* Develop an outline or use a graphic organizer to guide the draft you will create in the upcoming lessons. Include only facts, details, examples, and quotations that clearly support your opinion. Write your opinion statement and outline on a separate sheet of paper or in a new document.

**Conventions**

### Commas with *Yes* and *No*

**DIRECTIONS** Answer the questions by writing *yes* or *no* and then providing details to elaborate on your response.

**1.** Did more than one European explorer try to find the Northwest Passage?

_____

_____

**2.** Did any of the European explorers ever find a way to sail across the Americas?

_____

_____

**3.** Is there a way for ships to sail across the Americas today?

_____

_____

 Students write routinely for a range of tasks, purposes, and audiences. Students practice various conventions of standard English.

Name _____

**DIRECTIONS** Write a sentence using each word.

personal     historic     inspire

_____

_____

_____

_____

**Write in Response to Reading**

Read page 41. Ynes Mexia and her team were trapped at the bottom of a deep gorge in Peru for three months. Do you think she should have spent that time looking for new plants? Use text evidence to support your opinion. Write your response below, on a separate sheet of paper, or in a new document.

_____

_____

_____

_____

_____

_____

Students demonstrate contextual understanding of Benchmark Vocabulary. Students read text closely and use text evidence in their written answers.

Name _____

### Making a Difference for Immigrants

People have been immigrating to America for hundreds of years. They have come for adventure, wealth, work opportunities, and to escape persecution. Often that's what they have found. They also often found themselves in unfamiliar surroundings and among people who didn't want them here. One inspiring company went out of its way to make life better for immigrants.

In the late nineteenth century, young John Michael Kohler immigrated to the United States from Austria with his family. Kohler grew up and married a woman whose father co-owned a successful business in the steel and iron works industry. Kohler then purchased the business from his father-in-law in 1873, and the Kohler Company was founded. The company soon manufactured bathtubs and bath fixtures near Sheboygan, Wisconsin, and continues to do so today.

Kohler needed a great many workers to make all those bathtubs, sinks, and toilets! Unlike many other companies of that time, which exploited immigrants for labor, the Kohler Company tried to provide a better life for its employees.

Many of Kohler's workers were Austrian immigrants, just like John Michael Kohler was. The company emphasized worker safety, medical care, and good wages. One of the company's priorities was to ensure that Kohler employees not only had pleasant working conditions but also decent living conditions. Kohler began transforming the Village of Kohler into one of the first planned communities in the Midwest. The town had many attractive features: green spaces, single and two-family homes, recreational facilities, and a school. Creating a company town helped the Kohler business attract and keep a stable workforce.

The Kohler Company still wanted to do more so it built the American Club, a dormitory for immigrant employees. Housing costs were minimal. Many unmarried Kohler employees stayed there until they saved enough to buy a house and send for their families. Employees took lessons in English, American history, and civics. Immigrant workers got a day off and transportation to the courthouse as a first step toward becoming citizens. Between 1900 and 1930, the Kohler Company helped at least 1,200 immigrant workers become citizens.

Immigrants may have very different reasons for coming here, but most arrive with high hopes. The Kohler Company made a difference in the lives of its immigrant workers who were trying to make a new and better life in a foreign land.

Students read text closely to determine what the text says.

**Gather Evidence** Underline the advantages that the Kohler Company employees had that many other immigrant workers in the United States did not.

**Gather Evidence: Extend Your Ideas** Circle the event from his past that motivated Kohler to make a better life for his employees.

**Ask Questions** Write two questions you would ask a historian about conditions for immigrants during this time period.

_____

_____

**Ask Questions: Extend Your Ideas** Write an additional question about immigrants that is answered in the text. Place brackets around the answer in the text.

_____

_____

**Make Your Case** What was the best thing John Michael Kohler did for his immigrant workers? Write a detail from the text that reflects your opinion.

_____

_____

**Make Your Case: Extend Your Ideas** Use additional evidence from the text to support your opinion. Discuss your results with a partner.

_____

_____

 Students read text closely to determine what the text says.

Name _____

**Draft an Editorial** On a separate sheet of paper or in a new document, draft the introduction and body paragraphs of your editorial. Remember to include a clearly stated opinion in the introduction, identify the reasons and evidence that best support your opinion, and refer to your outline or graphic organizer to arrange reasons and evidence logically.

**Conventions**

## Commas with Tag Questions

**DIRECTIONS** Write a dialogue between two speakers about Chapters 5 and 6 of *Explorers of North America*. Each line of dialogue should contain a tag question. Write each line of dialogue on a separate line. Then identify whether the tag question in each line of dialogue is affirmative or negative.

1. _____

   _____

2. _____

   _____

3. _____

   _____

4. _____

   _____

Students write routinely for a range of tasks, purposes, and audiences. Students practice various conventions of standard English.

Name _____

**DIRECTIONS** Write a sentence using each word.

     wondrous    infernal    imploring    rebelled    intentions

_____

_____

_____

_____

_____

_____

**Write in Response to Reading**

Read pages 16–17 of *Beyond the Horizon* and pages 10–11 of *Explorers of North America*. How does the text structure in each of these sections present information on traveling to Asia? Use evidence from each text to support your explanation. Write your response below, on a separate sheet of paper, or in a new document.

_____

_____

_____

_____

_____

Students demonstrate contextual understanding of Benchmark Vocabulary. Students read text closely and use text evidence in their written answers.

## Narrative and Nonfiction Structures

**DIRECTIONS** Using evidence from the texts, answer the following questions about *Beyond the Horizon* and *Explorers of North America*.

1. How are the structures of the two texts similar?

   _____

   _____

2. How are the structures of the two texts different?

   _____

   _____

   _____

   _____

3. How does the structure of *Beyond the Horizon* help readers better understand the topic of exploration?

   _____

   _____

   _____

4. How does the structure of *Explorers of North America* help readers better understand the topic of exploration?

   _____

   _____

   _____

Students analyze and respond to literary and informational text.

Name _____

**Draft an Editorial**  On a separate sheet of paper or in a new document, draft  the counterargument and conclusion for your editorial. Refer to the outline you developed in Lesson 12. Include a clearly stated counterargument, using reasons and evidence to explain why the counterargument is flawed. End with a strong conclusion that restates the opinion, summarizes the editorial's key points, proposes an answer or solution, and includes a call to action.

### Commas to Indicate Direct Address

**DIRECTIONS**  Write a sentence to respond to each prompt. Directly address the person referred to in each prompt.

1.  Ask a classmate about his or her opinion of one of the texts from this unit.

    _____

    _____

2.  Ask a different classmate about a plot event in *Beyond the Horizon*.

    _____

    _____

3.  Tell  your teacher which explorer from *Explorers of North America* you liked best and why you liked him or her.

    _____

    _____

 Students write routinely for a range of tasks, purposes, and audiences. Students practice various conventions of standard English.

Name _____

**DIRECTIONS** Write a sentence using each word.

benefit    civilization    indentured

_____

_____

_____

_____

Which images best convey the main ideas in the text? Support your opinion with text evidence. Write your response below, on a separate sheet of paper, or in a new document.

_____

_____

_____

_____

_____

_____

Students demonstrate contextual understanding of Benchmark Vocabulary. Students read text closely and use text evidence in their written answers.

Name _____

**Revise or Rewrite an Editorial** Choose a partner to review and suggest revisions to your editorial. Revise your own draft based on your partner's feedback. Use a separate sheet of paper or start a new document.

**Conventions**

## Underlining and Italics for Titles of Works

**DIRECTIONS** On the lines in items 1–3, write an original sentence that includes a specific title from the category of work identified.

1. book _____

_____

2. magazine _____

_____

3. newspaper _____

_____

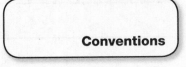

Students write routinely for a range of tasks, purposes, and audiences. Students practice various conventions of standard English.

Name _____

## Homographs

**DIRECTIONS**  Read each sentence. The words in parentheses are homographs, because they have different pronunciations and meanings. Use context and, if you wish, a dictionary to determine the meanings. On the line, write the definition of the word that makes sense in the sentence.

**1.** Matt used the sticky (compound, compound) to put the vase back together.

_____

**2.** Bella decided to (attribute, attribute) the success of the play to its director.

_____

**3.** The prisoners voted to (rebel, rebel) against their captors.

_____

**4.** Pat (resent, resent) the letter that had gotten lost.

_____

**5.** The transit employee said their bus passes were (invalid, invalid).

_____

**6.** It took Morris years to (perfect, perfect) her playing style.

_____

**7.** Darius set the tray on the (console, console).

_____

**8.** The children were amazed at the variety of (produce, produce) in the market.

_____

**9.** The fawns stood in a group near the (does, does).

_____

**10.** The (contrast, contrast) between light and dark is very sharp in the photo.

_____

Students apply grade-level phonics and word analysis skills.

Name _____

**DIRECTIONS** Write a sentence using each word.

profitable     attract

_____

_____

_____

_____

**Write in Response to Reading**

Write two or three paragraphs that explain the role of tobacco in the historical relationship between Native Americans and colonists in Virginia. Write your response below, on a separate sheet of paper, or in a new document.

_____

_____

_____

_____

_____

Students demonstrate contextual understanding of Benchmark Vocabulary. Students read text closely and use text evidence in their written answers.

**Edit and Proofread an Editorial**  Exchange drafts with a partner, and edit and proofread your partner's draft. Review the suggestions you receive from your partner and make corrections. Then write the edited version of your editorial on a separate sheet of paper or in a new document.

**Conventions**

## Quotation Marks for Titles of Works

**DIRECTIONS**  On the lines in items 1–5, write original sentences that include the titles of short works, such as songs, stories, and poems. Then identify the type of short work by writing it in parentheses next to the sentence.

1. _____

_____

2. _____

_____

3. _____

_____

4. _____

_____

5. _____

_____

Students write routinely for a range of tasks, purposes, and audiences. Students practice various conventions of standard English.

Name _____

**DIRECTIONS** Write a sentence using each word.

treaty    historic    benefit    civilization    profitable

_____

_____

_____

_____

_____

_____

_____

**Write in Response to Reading**

Write two paragraphs using text evidence from *Beyond the Horizon, Explorers of North America,* and *New Beginnings: Jamestown and the Virginia Colony* to support or disprove the following statement: *The rewards of exploration outweigh the risks.* Write your response below, on a separate sheet of paper, or in a new document.

_____

_____

_____

_____

_____

 Students demonstrate contextual understanding of Benchmark Vocabulary. Students read text closely and use text evidence in their written answers.

## Multiple Accounts

**DIRECTIONS** Using evidence from the texts, answer the following questions about *Beyond the Horizon, Explorers of North America,* and *New Beginnings: Jamestown and the Virginia Colony.*

1. Based on *Beyond the Horizon* and *Explorers of North America*, how are the challenges faced by traders and explorers alike and different?

   _____

   _____

   _____

   _____

2. Based on *Explorers of North America* and *New Beginnings*, how are the challenges faced by explorers and colonists alike and different?

   _____

   _____

   _____

3. How does each text present the idea that exploration has both benefits and drawbacks?

   _____

   _____

   _____

   _____

   _____

   _____

Students analyze and respond to literary and informational text.

**Publish and Present an Editorial**  Publish your editorial in a classroom newspaper. This may be a printed newspaper prepared with desktop publishing software, a poster display of the editorials, or an electronic newspaper or newsletter.

**Conventions**

## Spelling Correctly: Suffixes

**DIRECTIONS**  Carefully read each word below, and rewrite it spelled correctly.

1. runing _____

2. grined _____

3. bater _____

4. stoped _____

5. bigest _____

6. tiping _____

 Students write routinely for a range of tasks, purposes, and audiences. Students practice various conventions of standard English.

Name _____

**DIRECTIONS** Write a sentence using each word.

ample  navigator  lodged

_____

_____

_____

_____

**Write in Response to Reading**

Write a brief scene in which Martha describes the events on the river to Uncle Enoch. Be sure to have her describe her feelings as a result of the incident. Write your response below, on a separate sheet of paper, or in a new document.

_____

_____

_____

_____

_____

Students demonstrate contextual understanding of Benchmark Vocabulary. Students read text closely and use text evidence in their written answers.

**Support a Viewpoint in an Opinion Essay** Review the three texts discussed in Lesson 17. Which do you think offers the most insight into the Hutchins family's situation in the play? Write a short opinion piece to answer the question. Be sure to support your opinion with reasons and evidence from the texts. Use a separate sheet of paper or start a new document.

**Conventions**

### Spelling Correctly: Suffixes

**DIRECTIONS** Carefully read each word below, and rewrite it spelled correctly.

1. replyed _____

2. accompanyment _____

3. obeing _____

4. destroied _____

5. staiing _____

6. beautyful _____

Students write routinely for a range of tasks, purposes, and audiences. Students practice various conventions of standard English.